Louis Gaston de Segur

Plain talk about the Protestantism of to-day

Louis Gaston de Segur

Plain talk about the Protestantism of to-day

ISBN/EAN: 9783741185342

Manufactured in Europe, USA, Canada, Australia, Japa

Cover: Foto ©Lupo / pixelio.de

Manufactured and distributed by brebook publishing software (www.brebook.com)

Louis Gaston de Segur

Plain talk about the Protestantism of to-day

PLAIN TALK

ABOUT THE

PROTESTANTISM OF TO-DAY.

FROM THE FRENCH

MGR. SEGUR.

BOSTON:
PATRICK DONAHOE.
1868.

Entered according to act of Congress, in the year 1868, by
PATRICK DONAHOE,
In the Clerk's office of the District Court for the District of Massachusetts.

Imprimatur,
    Joannes Josephus,
        Episcopus Boston.

NOTE TO THE PUBLISHER.

You ask me, dear sir, "what makes me so anxious to publish this work in America?" — Well! I wish to have it published for the sake of Catholic children attending common schools, — of Catholic girls living out in families, — of Catholic boys serving their time, — of all dear and poor friends so often wounded in the affections dearest to their hearts, and whose religion is so often attacked in rude words.

I herewith hope to place in their hands such arms as they can easily use, and will have a telling effect on the enemies of their faith.

Nineteen editions have been published in France, up to 1866, and *six hundred thousand* copies sold.

The original title of the book is *Causeries*, — a word of difficult translation; *Conversations* does not render its precise meaning. Should any of your friends think of a more appropriate title-page, I shall be most thankful for the suggestion.

Reverend Mr. Faye, a Protestant minister at Lyons, has publicly complained of the *evils* caused by this little book. In 1859, before the Assembly of Protestant Bible-carriers held in Geneva, he solemnly avowed that "Protestants can never do any good (?) with *those who have read this book.*" — A parson of Poitiers acknowledged the same almost in the same terms; and we know of Catholics who, having incautiously admitted doubts about their faith, became reassured by reading this *plain talk.* — The wife of a minister in Paris returned the book to a lady friend with the remark that, "after reading it she could remain a Protestant no longer; she must consult her husband about it."

Not long ago an estimable English lady learned the truth of *the* Church from this work, became a Catholic, and, on her death-bed, directed that this little book should be laid on her breast in her coffin.

God bless the Author!

PLAIN TALK

PART FIRST.

I. WHY THIS LITTLE BOOK? — My *plain talk on Protestantism* is with Catholics, rather than with Protestants. It is not an attack, nor a controversy either; it is intended as a work of *preservation and self-defence.*

The question is often put, — what use to talk of Protestantism in these our times? Protestantism, we are told, has melted away into rationalism and infidelity, so that it has lost all its individuality as a religious sect. On the other hand, people have too much good sense, are too logical, to let it make an impression on them.

Protestantism is not genial; of its religious nature it shows naught but the ruins. But the mere existence of these ruins is a source of annoyance, for, however dismal they appear, they still afford a refuge to the wicked who dare not show themselves on the highways. Such is the dilapidated close of Protestantism within which the enemies of the Church gather every day more and more; they are joined by revolutionists and unbelievers. It covers, with an easy protection, their anarchical and impious plottings. All revolts against church and society are there fostered; and thus those ruins are transformed into citadels, and expiring Protestantism thus becomes a great power of destruction.

Revived and reanimated by impious spirits, which nestle in its bosom, it casts off piece after piece the cumbrous weight of theological armor, with which it was covered in the sixteenth century, and reveals in its nakedness its essential principle of rebelliousness. Retaining, for its particular purposes, a biblical cant and some religious forms, Protestantism stalks before us in the attitude of an aggressive power. It aims at nothing less than the total destruction of the Church of JESUS CHRIST; and to attain this end it multiplies churches, chapels, and establishments of all kinds in the midst of Catholic populations. Its colporteurs or carriers glut our towns and country with tracts. Here it endeavors to pervert the intelligence of the educated with periodicals, philosophical or literary publications. There an avenue is opened through the working classes, by entrapping their children. Schools, asylums, and *homes* are opened for them: therein the unfortunate little ones are not taught the way to become Christians, but how to blaspheme the Church. Numberless associations are formed,—they wage a war against the Catholic religion. We learn from the annual reports of biblical, evangelical, and other societies, the working and progress of their propagandism; they parade before us, with an air of triumph, the millions contributed by their party spirit, in all countries, to feed their zeal and reward their success.

Hence it cannot be an idle thing to occupy ourselves about Protestantism. Timid souls will object that there is no good in raising annoying disputes; we reply that not only we have a right, but it becomes our *duty* to defend the religion which is assailed, and to protect that which is to us dearer than life, the Faith we have received from GOD, and from our fathers. This small book will contribute its small efforts to this great work. I cannot but think that many souls will greatly profit by being shown, in a series of conversations in very plain talk, what Protestantism is; how false and hollow its system, how opprobrious its origin, its inefficiency as a religious worship, its affinity with rebellion and anarchy; and, lastly, how it must, without fail, lead people to an abyss of self destruction.

These pages will not contain elaborate disquisitions, nor metaphysical researches. I address myself to Catholics: they know their religion, and, hence, I do not insist on those points of doctrine which are well known, and which I would explain more at length, were I to address Protestants.

The question of the *Reformation* led me through a vast number of works, edited by Lutherans, Calvinists, Methodists, etc. I have met with extraordinary avowals on the part of Protestant pastors and writers, and have quoted those among them who are the most honored by their co-religionists.

This book may perhaps provoke recrimination on the part of Protestants. I cannot therefore insist enough on the fact that I stand here only to *defend* the Faith against attacks, the violence whereof surpasses all belief. There exist men who loudly proclaim to have received the mission of destroying our holy religion: one of their acknowledged leaders, Agenor de Gasparin, uttered the following language in regard to the Catholic Church: "*It is not allowed before God, to hate her only half way.*" (Les Ecoles du doute et l'ecole de la foi, p. 26.)

II. Proteus was a fabulous being who could assume all appearances, and thereby escaped research and attacks.

Proteus is the real type of what is called Protestantism. One is at a loss how to define it; it is almost impossible to lay one's hands upon it. It appears under different forms at Paris, and at London, in Geneva, and in Berlin, at Berne, or at New York. Aye more, it varies in every ward of a city, in every church, in the head of every minister, and, we may say it, in the mind of every Protestant. Here it teaches, says, and believes what elsewhere it denied, point blank: yet it is Protestantism everywhere.

What is, then, Protestantism?

Is it a religion?—No, it is only a collection of sects.

Is it a Church, or a conglomeration of Churches? —No, Protestantism is the individual.

Is it an institution?—No, it is a rebellion.

Is it an instruction?—No, it is a negation.

Protestantism *protests;* it goes no farther. The name is merely a negation; and this explains why the name has lasted for three hundred years, albeit the changes of Protestantism are numberless. Protestantism being only a renunciation of the ancient Christian Faith, the less it believes, the more it *will protest,* and the more will it prove true to its name. Its name becomes truer every day it shall live, to the last moment of the existence of Protestantism; then it will die, like the cancer, which is extinguished with the last bit of the flesh it has devoured.

Nevertheless, the fable tells us that Proteus was caught at last. Let us try to do the same, and surprise Protestantism under its thousand forms. Let us try to unmask it, and thus forearm the Christian, around whom it lays its snares.

III. PROTESTANTISM AND PROTESTANTS. — Are *Protestantism and Protestants* one and the same thing?—Not at all. Protestants are men beloved of GOD like every other man. But Protestantism is a rebellion against truth, a rebellion which GOD detests, and curses upon earth, as he detested and cursed the rebellion of the angels in heaven. We must love the Protestant, but detest Protestantism; as we must love the sinner, but detest sin.

Protestantism is an evil in its nature. A Protestant is often a very brave man, always immensely above his Protestantism. Generally speaking, he is a Protestant only in name, and the want of religion in him is frequently a consequence of his education, and of his associations, rather than a personal and culpable sentiment.

In my *plain talk* I do not attack Protestants, I attack Protestantism, which I brand as the arch-enemy of souls. Above all, I pity poor Protestants, a majority of whom are, I believe, in good faith. GOD will show them mercy, if, in the midst of this great disaster, which is called *Protestantism*, they honestly endeavor to find out the way of truth.

Protestantism is a deceitful doctrine. Out upon all error!

A Protestant is a man for whom our Saviour has suffered, and for him he died as for every other man: he is a brother whom we are bound to love.

IV. CATHOLICITY AND CATHOLICS.—*Protestantism and Protestants* are not one and the same thing; nor are *Catholicity and Catholics* the same and one.

Protestantism is in all cases worse than Protestants. This is absolutely true, and it can be easily understood. The sinner is always better than his sin: the man who is deceived is better than his error. Sin and error are, in fact, absolutely and essentially evil; but the man who either sins, or is misled, has always some good quality, some remnant of truth, and purity of heart.

Not so with Catholicity, which is always better than the Catholics. Let the Catholic be ever so good, perfect, even a saint, he will always retain some of the imperfections of human frailty and the traces of original sin. The Catholic Church guides her follower in the ways of God, points truth to him, and is free of all alloy, and absolutely good. The Church always teaches perfect sanctity, and is therefore always superior to its disciple.

Protestant ministers, in their attacks against the Church, often confound the Catholic with Catholicity. They make no distinction between the disciple, who is always imperfect, and the doctrine, which is perfect. Hence the unjust recrimination, and often ill-feelings; and hence also obstacles, chimerical it is true, but powerful enough to prevent a return to truth.

V. CATHOLICS AND CATHOLICS — PROTESTANTS AND PROTESTANTS. — "Things of the same sort are not alike" (*il y a fagots et fagots*), quoth the woodman in the play. It is even so in this question: let us make further distinction.

Catholics are not all alike. We must distinguish between Catholic and Catholic: the genuine Catholic and the contraband Catholic. There is the earnest Catholic, who can give an account of his religion, follow its dictates with his whole heart, fulfil the duties of prayer and self-denial, be assiduous in works of charity, and seek a close union with our Lord. Again, there are Catholics only in name, who are indifferent about their religion, never pray, never approach the sacraments, neglect the service of God. Be on your guard, lest you confound the *two* together; never take a bad Catholic as the type of Catholics in general.

Nor are Protestants all alike. Some Protestants are ardent, ever ready for a fight against the Church, prompted by motives of sect and propagandism. Others among them are Protestants because they were born such: they care very little for what their ministers say, and, in fact, cannot even tell to which of the thousand and one Protestant sects they belong. Let us not confound these two classes together. The former are sectarians and sworn enemies; in their blind zeal they will disguise themselves in every possible way to attain their mischievous purpose; and it becomes necessary to tear the mask from them and challenge them. The latter are simply in a dormant state; they are neither friendly nor hostile to the truth; they need only to be roused and bring the truth to glare on their eyes.

To the former class belong all those for whom Protestantism is a position, if not a profession. With them we must class also a small number of Protestants, especially those who are enthusiastic, who pay their agents largely, and look upon prices as a party concern.

The latter class reckons among its number, with few exceptions, a crowd of mechanics, merchants, and good-natured people, who are Protestants because their parents were such before them. Their religion is that of honest people; and in that they are very much like bad Catholics.

Without establishing this twofold distinction, we could not pave our way for our *Plain Talk*.

VI. HOW IT HAPPENS THAT THERE ARE PROTESTANTS REALLY GOOD AND STRONGLY RELIGIOUS. —We have Catholics, who bring shame upon their religion, who belong to the body of the Church, yet do not breathe her spirit. Thus, also, there are outside the pale of Catholicity separated brethren, Protestants, who yet do lead a Christian life, and follow the precepts of the Gospel. They belong, to a certain degree, to the spirit of the Church, and whatever faith and virtue their fine souls possess, it is all the property of Catholicity. They are Catholic at heart, and the Church looks upon them with tenderness. They are good Christians, as the word goes, not *because* they are Protestants, but *in spite* of their being Protestants.

Protestantism is only a negation, and can give them nothing. Its influence is limited to depriving them of that portion of religious resources which they would have, had they received their birth in the bosom of the Catholic Church.

An absolute certainty in matters of faith, a perfect and vivifying worship, the sanctifying consolations of the sacraments of Penance and Eucharist, and devotion to our Blessed Lady, and so many other resources supplied by the Catholic Church, would render these correct and virtuous Protestants immensely better. With the aid of these powerful means they would become saints. Deprived, as they are, of these aids, they have no lofty aspirations, and their piety, however real it may appear, never rises above a common level.

Our saints are, after all, only *good Catholics*. But what a difference there exists between such as a Saint Vincent of Paul, a Saint Francis of

Sales, a Saint Francis Xavier, a Saint Teresa, and those honest and honorable men, whose life is often quoted for a proof of the truth of Protestantism!

Lavater, a Protestant minister, in his *Letter to the Count of Stolberg*, remarks: "The Catholics have saints, I cannot deny it, and we have none; at least none that are like the Catholic."

VII. WHY ARE THERE MORE BAD CATHOLICS THAN BAD PROTESTANTS?—First, because the number of Catholics is far superior to that of Protestants. In a large city, like Boston, there must be, of course, more bad people than in Brookline or Hull.

Again, the Catholic religion is very earnest in enjoining upon us, on the part of God, a precise and obligatory belief, many noble duties, a determined worship and well-defined and indispensable means of sanctification.

This is all divine, it is true, but it is arduous nevertheless, and human passions do not find their interest in it. The Catholic catechism foresees all and leaves naught to hap-hazard. It is not satisfied with a vague and vapid religiousness; its dots the *i* (as the French proverb has it), and tells you most explicitly what you must do, and what you shall not do, under penalty of proving yourself a bad Catholic. It commands the practice of exterior observances, which are irksome, because they clash with our corrupt inclinations. Abstinence, fast, confession, etc., etc., must be irksome, of course. One must needs have great energy and great perseverance to keep within the limits of this narrow path.

It is not so on the broad way, or rather on the boundless desert, over which Protestant sects wish us to wander. Certainly, especially at the present time, the religious baggage of Protestantism is not very heavy. Nothing is easier than to be a good Protestant. It is not I who say so, but one of the best known and and most stirring parsons of Paris. Tracing the character of a writer,* whose panegyric he draws, and whom he introduces to us as an excellent Protestant, he says: "Of dogmas *he believed very little* .... As for truth, he knew not how to look for it in the dogma, or *even in the Gospel.* He believed that there was a germ of truth in the holy Scriptures; but he believed them to be mixed up with all kinds of errors, and fancied that with their aid we might

* Mr. de Sismondi, Protestant historian. See the *Journal of Lien.*

maintain and prove everything alike .... *He believed little in prayer* .... HE HEARTILY DETESTED CATHOLICITY." There you have the Christian. That *will do.* There you have the Protestant, according to the minister Coquerel.

You see, dear reader, 'tis not very hard to be a good Protestant. Believe whatever you choose in matters of religion. Believe nothing at all, if it suits you better. Be honest, as the world understands it. Read the Bible or not, as it pleases you; go to church or do not go; forget not to subscribe to one or two or three Bible and Evangelical societies; but, above all, hold the Catholic Church in abomination,—and you shall be a good Protestant.*

We shall now quote the opinion of Count de Stolberg, an illustrious Protestant, and a convert to the Catholic Church: it will come with more grace from his own mouth:—

"I have always observed that the worst Catholics become very easily the best of Protestants, and even parsons; but it is my every day's experience that a good Protestant, such

---

* J. J. Rousseau says of the Protestants of Neufchâtel that, "In their estimation, he is a Christian who goes to hear the sermon every Sunday: during the interval he may do as he pleases."—*Lettre au Maréchal de Luxembourg.*

as I was, finds it a very hard work to become even a passable Catholic."

Were we not following close the Protestant ministers, and were we not reading their writings, we would scarcely believe the religious nothingness which lies concealed under the convenient cloak of Protestantism. The unprincipled Eugene Sue exclaimed with great truth, on the sight of this facility, that "the surest means to *unchristianize* Europe was to *Protestantize* it."

VIII. PROTESTANTISM IS SEPARATED FROM THE CHURCH BY AN ABYSS. — The agent of Protestant propagandism generally opens his way to an unsophisticated and ignorant mind with the remark, that "Protestant or Catholic, it is almost all the same!" And Catholics are to be found who echo this blasphemy, without the least thought that thereby they offer a grave insult to the Church, their mother.

You say Protestantism, with its myriads of subdivisions, is *about* the same as the Catholic Church! Do you understand yourself? You might as well say that counterfeit money is *about* as valuable as good coin.

Where the Church affirms, the Protestant denies; where the Church teaches, the Protestant revolts. In the Catholic Church, the unity of faith, worship, and religion, is fundamental and perfect. Among the Protestants, every man believes as he chooses, and acts as he believes: theirs is religious anarchy, an opposition to unity. They agree on only one point, — hatred of Catholicity.

The distinct, infallible teachings of the Church are the rule of faith for a Catholic. The Protestant rejects the Church, despises her authority, and takes for his guidance only the Bible, which he interprets as he best may, or as he chooses.

The Catholic reveres the Pope as the vicar of Jesus Christ, the head of the faithful, the chief pastor, the infallible doctor of the law. But the Protestant looks upon him only as the anti-Christ, Satan's vicar, and the arch-enemy of the gospel.

The Catholic adores Jesus Christ really present in the Eucharist; the Protestant sees in it only an empty symbol, a piece of bread.

The Catholic reveres, invokes, loves the Holy Virgin Mary, mother of GOD. The Protestant feels for her an estrangement so insuperable, that it often exhibits itself in contempt, and even in hatred.

The Catholic draws his Christian vitality from the seven sacraments of the Church, and supports it chiefly by approaching the sacraments of Penance and Eucharist. The Protestant does not recognize these sacraments; aye, few are the sects that preserve a true conception of Baptism.

And so on with all the dogmas. Yes, I say *all*, even the most essential to the nature of religion, such dogmas without which there cannot be a Christian. The farther one advances, the more Protestantism will *protest* against the faith he has abandoned. In Geneva, Strasburg, Paris, — in almost all the theological faculties of French, German, American Protestants, — their ministers deny the divinity of our Lord Jesus Christ, deny the mystery of the holy Trinity, and original sin, and sap the very foundations of Christianity.

The Protestant sects *about* the same as the holy Catholic Church, indeed! They are all separated from it, more or less, according as they are more or less logical, and apply more strictly the Protestant principle of private interpretation. And those sects which still seem to bear some resemblance to the Church, are none the less separated from her by a wide abyss.

IX. CAN CATHOLICITY AND PROTESTANTISM BE BOTH EQUALLY TRUE? — Evidently no.

Religion is the knowledge and service of the one true GOD; hence it must be *one*, as GOD is. One GOD, one Truth, one Christ, one Faith, one Religion.

Whoever asserts that the true religion of Christ is in Protestantism as well as in Catholicity, and *vice versa*, is either an infidel, that cares very little about truth, or an ignorant man, who talks at random.

If two religions which are diametrically opposed, such as the Catholic on one side, and the sects on the other, could be equally true, we must admit that both YES and NO can be asserted as equally true on any question upon which two disputants may happen to join opposite issues.

I have given proofs of the fundamental opposition which exists between the Catholic Church and the different fractions of Protestantism. Let us re-quote one:—

The Church teaches that our Lord JESUS CHRIST is really, truly, and substantially in the Eucharist. The Protestant sects deny this, and charge the Church with idolatry. In sooth, one of the two must be false. But a religion which is wrong, even in only one point, cannot be the true one. Therefore it is simply impossible that Catholicity and Protestantism should both be true.

X. KEEP ON THE SAFEST SIDE.—Melancthon, the favorite desciple of Luther, had prevailed on his mother to follow him in the path of the so-called Lutheran Reformation. On her deathbed she called her son, and solemnly charged him to tell her the truth:—

"My son, by thy urgency I have abandoned the Catholic Church, and followed the new religion. I am about appearing before GOD, and I adjure thee by the living GOD, tell me, and keep not the truth from me,—in what faith must I die?"

Melancthon bent his head, and was silent for a while. There was a struggle in his heart between love for his mother and the pride of sectarianism. But at last he made answer:—

"Mother, the Protestant doctrine is the easiest, but the Catholic is *the surest!*"*

Then, if the Catholic religion is the surest, surely one should embrace it, and much more never abandon it to embrace a less safe one.

This simple argument, based on good sense, determined Henry IV. to become a Catholic. A conference on religion was going on in Saint

---

* Andin, Life of Luther, t. III. p. 288.

Denis, before the king and his court. On one side many Catholic doctors; on the other, the ministers Duverdier, Morlas, Salette, and some others.

The historian Perefixe tells us that "The king, observing that none of the Protestant divines dared to deny that one may be saved in the Catholic Church, remarked: 'What! you are all of one accord in that there is salvation in the Roman Church?' 'Certainly,' rejoined the minister, 'provided a man leads a good life.' Then, turning to the Catholic doctors, 'do you think, gentlemen,' he asked, 'that I can work out my salvation remaining a Protestant?' 'It is our belief, sire, and we solemnly profess it before you, that having once known the true Church, you must enter it, and that there is no salvation for your soul if you remain a Protestant.'

"Whereupon the king judiciously remarked, in addressing the ministers: It is then the behest of prudence that I should belong to the religion of the Catholics, and not to yours. For, you agree with them that in their religion I can be saved; whereas, in yours, I can be saved, it is true, in your opinion, but not in theirs. According to prudence, then, I must keep on the safest side."

And he became a Catholic.

XI. Is Heresy a great Sin? — Heresy is one of the greatest crimes a child of God can be guilty of. It is an apostasy from the Church.

Faith is the foundation of all religious edifices, — the first element of Christian life. Accordingly, our Lord sums up the whole system of religion in faith. At every page of his gospel he repeats that to be saved it is necessary to *believe* in him, to *believe* in his word, to *believe* in the word of the Church.

HE THAT BELIEVETH AND IS BAPTIZED SHALL BE SAVED; BUT HE THAT BELIEVETH NOT SHALL BE CONDEMNED. (Mark xvi. 16.)

Heresy is a sin against faith. It is a deliberate and obstinate rebellion against the divine teachings of the Church of JESUS CHRIST. Heresy subverts the order established by GOD, and separates man from the great Catholic family which, on earth and in heaven, is the family of GOD.

Hence, heresy is in itself a more grievous sin, an evil far greater and more baneful, than immorality and the inordinations of sensuality. These disorders and sins are very bad, indeed, and separate a great many from JESUS CHRIST; but they do not inflict upon the soul an inordination so radical and so dangerous as heresy.

We have, then, the criterion whereby to

judge the religious responsibility and heavy culpability of those evangelical ministers who sow heresy around them. They inflict upon society an evil far worse than the emissaries of libertinism can inflict.

XII. WHETHER A PROTESTANT CAN BE SAVED. — Certainly he can. But let us understand each other well.

"One may be in *error;* but that is far different from being in *heresy.*" Such was the distinction of Saint Augustine instructing his people on the possible salvation of heretics. Indeed, one can be deceived without being aware of it. An *involuntary* material *error* is a misfortune, not a sin. Hence one may be saved in error. But heresy is a rebellion against GOD and his Church; it is a sin; it is a crime, — and, therefore, one cannot be saved in heresy.

This is tantamount to say that *only an* INVINCIBLE *good faith* can excuse a Protestant from the sin of heresy, and afford him, in his misfortune, a possibility of salvation.

But where this good faith does not exist, the heretic is lost, because he parts company with truth, which is JESUS, and from the association of truth, which is the Catholic, apostolic, and Roman Church.

But are there Protestants in good faith? Can this *invincible*, good faith be said to exist in countries where the Catholic religion is well known, — in the midst of Catholics, — where the opportunities to find the Church are so abundant? God alone can fathom this mystery; He alone can judge it.

To judge from appearances, we are led to think that this *good faith* is very often to be found among Protestants, and, above all, among those who belong to the working classes, debarred as they are from the means of instruction, — that instruction, the working whereof renders the learned classes inexcusable. I must confess, that, even admitting the absolute *possibility* of this wonder, I have not the least trust in the *good faith* of ministers, and that I greatly fear for their eternal welfare.

As regards Protestants in *good faith*, — *bona fide* Protestants, such as can be saved, — I must add a qualification, which will make us even more apprehensive of their danger. Their salvation, although possible, is nevertheless much more difficult for them than for us Catholics.

· I will tell you why. — At first, the faith of a Protestant is always more or less uncertain.

But faith is the starting-point, the vivifying principle of those Christian virtues, with whose aid one can save his soul. The faith of the Catholic is clear, defined, and free from all the whims of his own mind.

Again: as I have said before, Protestants do not partake of the resources which the Church affords to her children, for the purpose of aiding them in leading such a life as will secure for them a right to heaven. The most powerful of these resources are the sacraments of confession and communion. Should the great misfortune of committing a mortal sin befall men, he cannot be reconciled with GOD but through the confession of his misdemeanors, and the absolution received at the hands of the priest. Should he, peradventure, be absolutely unable to go to confession, it becomes necessary for him to join to a heartfelt wish for the sacrament the deepest sorrow, and the purest and noblest love, which is defined — *perfect contrition*. The very fact that this contrition must be perfect renders it very difficult and very rare. This contrition is desirable in all cases, but it is not indispensable, when the sacrament of penance is approached; in which case, an ordinary repentance will suffice; for, in this sacrament of mercy, our Lord vouchsafes to forgive the deficiencies of the poor penitent.

The Protestant who has committed sin has not at his command the healing aid of confession. He must then have recourse to perfect contrition, — the result of a perfect sorrow for sin, and a pure love of God; without which he can obtain neither remission of his sin nor eternal salvation. He cannot unite to this contrition the wish of going to confession, because I suppose him to be *bona fide*, in good faith, and accordingly ignorant of the necessity of this sacrament. *Therefore*, it becomes by far more difficult for him, than for the Catholic, to become reconciled with GOD.

But, suppose even that, by a favor most special, he succeeds in conceiving this perfect contrition, he is still deprived of the holy communion, which has been instituted by our Saviour precisely for the purpose of nourishing us with spiritual food, protecting us against sin, if we are innocent; preserving us from falling again into it, if, after having indulged in it, we are relieved and purified. In holy communion we have, as it were, the food necessary to support us during our journey through life. The poor Protestant has not this food, and runs great risk of becoming faint in his journey.

Hence, it becomes difficult for him to be sanctified and saved.

Thus, it becomes our duty to make an effort for his conversion, and thereby place him in the way of securing chances to find, and more powerful aids to secure, that which is, after all, the *only* end for which we have been placed in this world.

XIII. THE DIFFERENCE BETWEEN CONVERSION AND APOSTASY. — Conversion is a duty, apostasy a crime. A Protestant entering the bosom of the Church becomes a convert. A Catholic deserting his Church to join a sect becomes an apostate. Why this difference?

Listen: The Catholic faith, as taught invariably for eighteen centuries, consists in a certain number of positive dogmas, such as the Unity of GOD, the Trinity, Incarnation, Real Presence, Papacy, etc., etc. To put it in round numbers, let us suppose these dogmas to amount to fifty. On this supposition, the Christians have, then, believed fifty dogmas to the beginning of the tenth century; up to which time there had been only *one* faith in Christendom. At that epoch, the Greeks denied the procession of the Holy Ghost from Father and Son, and the supremacy of the Holy See, and thus they have maintained only forty-eight out of the fifty dogmas of the Church. Hence it is evident that we Catholics have always believed all that the Greek Church believes, whilst she, on her part, denies two of these dogmas, which we do believe.

In the sixteenth century the Protestants pushed things a great deal farther, and denied still more dogmas. Some denied twenty of them, and some thirty; others admitted hardly any. But, however, more or less they may retain we own all they do own. The Catholic Church believes all that the Protestant Churches do believe. There is no controversy on this point.

But then, these sects, whatever name they go by, are not *religious*, because they have been formed only by denying this or that dogma. They are only *negations;* which means they are nothing in themselves, because from the moment they *assert* they become Catholic.

Hence follows a consequence, a striking evidence in itself, to wit: the Catholic who steps over to a Protestant sect does truly *apostatize*, inasmuch as he abandons a belief, and denies to-day what he believed yesterday. At the same time the Protestant, who enters the pale of the Catholic Church does not cast off any dogma, he does not deny anything he believed before; on the contrary, he believes what he denied, which makes a great difference: which argument is borrowed from Count de Maistre.

In 1813, De Joux, a Protestant minister of Geneva, afterwards president of the reformed consistory of Nantes, uttered these words: "For my part, I should blame a Catholic who became Protestant, because it is not right that he who possesses the most should go in quest of the less. But I could not blame a Protestant who became Catholic, because it is fair that he who has the least should aspire after the most."

In 1825, De Joux became a Catholic.

XIV. WHY DO SOME BECOME PROTESTANTS, AND OTHERS BECOME CATHOLICS?—1. Except in very rare cases, which are *always* explained by a profound ignorance both of the Catholic religion which is abandoned, and of Protestantism which is embraced, I maintain that never did a Catholic become Protestant from Christian and accountable motives.

I have known many so-called Catholics who wished to become Protestant. One of them, an intelligent and amiable youth was desperately in love with the daughter of a Protestant minister; hence he ardently wished to become

Protestant. It was decidedly the most *disinterested* conviction of the excellence of Protestantism.

Then I knew a priest who had foresworn all his duties and led a disorderly life. His bishop was obliged to suspend him from his ecclesiastical functions . . . . to-day he is a Protestant minister.

A third proselyte, a young German instructress, felt humbled at being constrained to live in a foreign family. Some Protestant friends offered her a situation of great ease, on condition that she would renounce her faith. I have it written to me in a letter by her own handwriting: "*Cost what it may*, I must have a home."

These are only a few instances of what occurs every day. The character of these pretended conversions is so well defined, that the Protestants are above all annoyed by them. One of them wrote that "Protestantism was the sewer of Catholicity." Dean Swift said that "when the Pope weeds his garden he throws the garbage over our walls;" which saying is now quoted as a proverb in England.

In the language of a Protestant Swiss journal "While the Catholic Church swells her ranks with Protestants well instructed, most intelligent, and the best for their morality, our Reformed Church can levy recruits only among lecherous and concubinarian monks." In fact Luther, Calvin, Zwinglius, Oecolampadius, Bucer, and many others were all ecclesiastics suspended for their crimes, unfrocked or bad monks; and since then every bad priest * that treads in their footsteps, will throw himself, as if by instinct, into the arms of Protestantism, and therein find sympathy and protection. They were the shame and dregs of the Catholic Church, and are transformed at once into ministers of the PURE Gospel. They are heard, honored, applauded. Moreover their apostasy

---

* As a specimen of this kind of conversions we shall here copy a fragment of a letter written, not long ago, to the Bishop of Breslau by the only priest known to have apostatized in Silesia: —

" . . . Inasmuch as my ecclesiastical superiors have not deigned to take into consideration the motives I have alleged for the purpose of being appointed to a charge corresponding to my abilities, I feel constrained, after having so long and in vain looked for preferment, and from *a spite* against such treatment, to return to primitive Christianity. Accordingly, I have resolved to take for my wife Mlle. Leontine Krause, who for some time past has kept house for me in a very disinterested manner

"(Signed) SCHULICH, *Demissionary Curate.*"

Poor man! wretched Protestantism doomed to become the asylum of such criminals and to legalize such sentiments!

is paraded, and the Protestant sects pride and feast on what holy Church rejects with loathing. The apostate monk Achilli, cast away from his convent and expelled from his native soil on account of his infamous libertinism, was received with an ovation in England.* Other wretches of the same cast have met with greeting and lucrative employment at the hands of Protestants in Geneva and Paris. Let the *Reformation* treasure these conquests. We give them up with a willing heart.

Not long ago, a Prussian lady, who had been a Catholic for about eight or ten years, thus replied with a sad candor to a clergyman, a friend of mine, who exhorted her to stand firm, as she seemed to be yielding to the entreaties and flattering offers of her family: "*I became a Catholic for the love of God; I am going to be a Protestant from love of myself!*" — The truest solution of the whole question.

One is poor, and wishes to emerge from his poverty; another is swayed by passions, which he does not wish to control; a third has too much pride, and is loath to subdue it; a fourth is ignorant, and allows himself to be led away. . . . For such reasons people become Protestant.

* V. Achilli vs. Newman. New York: Dewitt & Davenport.

2. It is quite different with those Protestants who become Catholic. — I allow that human motives may have sometimes influenced a Protestant to enter the Church. But such cases form only an imperceptible exception. We have seen, on the faith even of Protestants, that those among them who become Catholic, are most honorable, most learned, and the most virtuous. Never was this fact more evident than in our own times.

During the last twenty years a vast number of Anglican ministers have adjured heresy in England. They were the cream of the universities of Great Britain, men of learning. Suffice it to name Newman, Manning, Faber, and Wilberforce. But then it is an every-day occurrence to hear of conversions from distinguished men of the clergy, nobility, army, and navy of England, and of America, recorded by the national papers in spite of themselves.

Take, for instance, the remarkable conversion of Lord Spencer, a British lord of the highest nobility. After becoming a Catholic, he enters the Congregation of Passionists, a most austere and most humble order, in which he was known by the name of Father Ignatius. While yet a Protestant, he endeavored to prevail on the Protestants of all classes to pray for the conversion of England, on condition, however, that if the Catholic Church was that of JESUS CHRIST, the Lord would vouchsafe to bring England back to that Church. After becoming a Catholic he continued with a persevering zeal in this crusade of prayer, which has been the source of so many graces to his country. (See *Catholic World*, New York, July, 1867.)

In Germany, instances of most illustrious conversions have been afforded especially in sovereign or princely families. In 1817, the Duke of Saxe-Gotha, a near relation of the King of England, re-entered the bosom of the Church, and by his fervid piety became the edification of Catholics as well as Protestants. In 1822, Prince Henry Edward of Schoenburg became a Catholic; and in 1826, the Count of Ingenheim, brother to the King of Prussia, Frederic, Duke of Mecklenburg, the Countess of Solms-Bareuth, Charlotte, Princess of Mecklenburg, wife to the Prince Royal of Denmark,* etc.,

---

* Many writers have published catalogues of the most celebrated conversions which have taken place in this century. See among them Rohrbacher: *Tableau des principales conversions qui ont eu lieu parmi les Protestants depuis le commencement du dix-neuvième siècle;* also from the pen of the same writer: *Motifs qui ont ramené à l'Eglise un grand nombre de Protestants.* — See ALZOG's *Histoire Universelle de l'Eglise*, t. III. § 406 and following.

etc., etc. Let us add to this catalogue of princely conversions that of the brother of the present King of Wurtemberg, which took place in Paris, in 1851.

Who has not heard of the Count Stolberg, one of the most eminent men at the beginning of this century? He became a convert in consequence of a close study of the authorities of the Bible, of the Fathers and of controversialists. Truth required at his hands a sacrifice of the hopes of a most brilliant career; but God consoled him with the conversion of his entire family.

Stolberg's example carried with it a host of German writers, philosophers, and jurists of the first class, who became reconciled with the Church. The conversion of the famous scholar, Werner, was, perhaps, the most remarkable. Having gained positions of the highest trust in Berlin, he gave them all up, to become a Catholic and a priest. He died in the Congregation of Redemptorists. They relate of him, that being once at a dinner with some highly distinguished Protestants, one of them, who could never forgive him for having abandoned the so-called Reformation, said before the guests that he never thought much of a man who had changed his religion. "Nor I either; and this is the very reason why I have always despised Luther," replied Werner.

Werner's example was followed by other scientists of the same nation, such as Frederick Schlegel, the Baron of Eckstein, the Aulic Councillor Adam Muller, etc., etc.

In Switzerland, Charles Louis de Haller, a patrician of Berne, and member of the Supreme Council, is one of the most illustrious Protestants that became Catholic in that confederacy. Like the majority of all those I have named above, he had the honor of being persecuted, deprived of all his titles and offices, and lastly exiled by the Protestants, whose *tolerance* is ever of the same stamp, whenever they can have their own way.

Haller's conversion was followed, in Switzerland, by that of the ministers Esslinger of Zurich, Pierre de Joux of Geneva, and of th' illustrious ecclesiastical president of the Consistory of Schaffhouse, Frederic Hurter. He made his profession of faith in Rome, in 1844, having for his godfather the great painter, Overbeck, himself a convert of some years' standing, whose life and virtues have been the object of so much edification in the Eternal City.

Nor has France been behindhand in giving

her quota of conversions from Protestantism, especially among ministers. That of Mr. Laval, pastor of Condè-sur-Noiveau, was the most remarkable. He was followed by Mr. Paul Latour, president of the Consistory of Maz-d'Asil.

Two years after, in 1846, the conversion of M. A. Bermaz took place in Lyons. He had, during four years, professed the doctrines of the *Mômiers*, and was zealously at work in promulgating them through the diocese of Lyons. But he abjured his errors and made known the motives of his conversion in a pamphlet published in Lyons.

And in our own days how many Protestants in name, how many parsons, above all, would willingly throw themselves into the arms of Holy Church, were it not for the ties of family and temporal interest? *Protestant consistories very cunningly hurry young pastors to be married immediately after leaving school.* Wife and children are the greatest obstacle to the conversion of a Protestant minister. Many an example I could quote to support this assertion.

America comes in also for her share in the number of noble, correct, and virtuous souls who have swollen the ranks of converts to Catholicity.

Suffice it to quote the conversion of the Protestant Bishop of North Carolina, Doctor Ives. It is well known how highly esteemed he was for his excellent character, learning and science. He sought the truth with an honest heart, and, as he found it, he abandoned all to possess it. The Protestant Bishop gave up his opulent bishopric, and undertook a journey to Rome, to throw himself at the feet of the Sovereign Pontiff. On the 26th of December, 1852, he made his profession of faith in the Pope's private chapel. Throwing himself on his knees before the Holy Father, he presented to him the ring and the seal, — the insignia of the eminent place he whilom occupied among the Protestants, and as he surrendered them with the cross he wore on solemn occasions, "Holy Father!" he said with tears, "*here are the marks of my rebellion!*" — "They shall be henceforward the token of your submission, and as such go and lay them on St. Peter's tomb," replied the Vicar of JESUS CHRIST.

Let now Protestantism set off its conquests against these men, so great for their virtues, their position, their love of truth! We shall not ask illustrious names, — men who for greatness of talent, or nobility of character, might offset those we have just named. Truly it has none: else they would have been proclaimed from the house-tops. Yet we would be satisfied were they to point to us, at least, some honest and virtuous, well *instructed* and *practical* Catholics, who have left our ranks, urged by the want of a better belief, and such as have edified their new sectaries with an exemplary life.*

I DEFY the Protestants to bring forward *even one*. The apostates who pass over to Protestantism are generally individuals who hope to better their fortune in a change of religion, or else sour spirits who wish to obtain revenge by giving scandal; while the Christians who emerge

* Not long ago a Protestant minister held with a priest of the French missions a conversation in a stage, which is well worth relating here. The minister, with resentful, albeit polite terms, was remonstrating with the missioner for the late recruits obtained out of the ranks of Protestantism. "But," answered the priest with a smile, "you have as many on your side." "Ah!" replied he, with great naivéte, "you give us your garbage, and take our cream." (*Foi et lumieres* 2d ed. p. 193.)

A writer quoted by Mr. Foisset, in his *Catholicity and Protestantism*, has said: "Had I the misfortune of not being Catholic, two things would disturb me, I must confess. The first, the number and superior mind of those who have believed in the Roman Church *after examination*, ever since the times of Luther and Calvin. Secondly, the number and superior mind of those who, *after examination*, have abandoned Luther and Calvin to go over to Rome. I would hence come to the conclusion that there is room for examination, and I WOULD examine."

from Protestant sects to enter the Church of Jesus Christ look for and indeed find a faith that is solid, clear, and definite, comfort, peace, holiness, and love.

I shall now, by way of conclusion, quote a well-known fact, the consideration whereof has already shaken many Protestant consciences. THERE IS SCARCELY A CATHOLIC PRIEST, HOWEVER LIMITED THE SPHERE OF HIS ACTION MAY BE, WHO HAS NOT BEEN CALLED TO RECEIVE INTO THE CHURCH A DYING PROTESTANT; WHILE THERE IS NO RECORD WHATEVER OF A SINCERE CATHOLIC WHO HAS WISHED TO BECOME PROTESTANT AT THE MOMENT HE WAS SUMMONED TO APPEAR BEFORE THE TRIBUNAL OF GOD.

Ignorance, bad passions, a forgetfulness of divine justice, goad unhappy souls to Protestantism.

A correct conscience, healthy learning, a love of truth, and the fear of God, lead souls back to the Catholic Church.

Draw your conclusions now.

XV. IS PROTESTANTISM AFTER ALL A RELIGION?—Perhaps I shock some one's sensitiveness by saying, no.

What is religion? It is a covenant of Doctrine and Worship which binds people together in one belief and in one uniform manner of serving God.—Thus, e. g., among false religions, are Judaism, Mahomedanism, Buddhism, etc.

Very well: Protestantism lays down as a fundamental principle that every man is perfectly free to *believe* as he chooses, and to serve God as he pleases. Therefore, Protestantism makes away with the very idea of *religion*, which implies *bond, union, unity*. I know very well that Protestants do not always draw the extreme and rigorous consequences of this principle. In Catholic countries, and above all in France, they keep up, as much as they can, the appearance of union among the different sects. But in Germany, for instance, in Switzerland, in America, where they have plenty of elbow-room, they actually *boast* of having as many beliefs as there are individuals.

Of all religious institutions, built by the hand of man, Protestantism is distinguished by this trait of destroying what constitutes the essence, I will not say of true religion, but of all religions in general. All false religions, in imitation of the true one, have a code of belief and worship, the rejection whereof excludes one from belonging thereto; whereas what the reverend gentlemen endeavor to pass for religion is but an anarchy without rule or restraint, which only denies, destroys, *protests:* it bears the mark of self-condemnation by appropriating the anti-religious title of *Protestantism.*

Never did Jean Jacques Rousseau utter a greater truth than when he said of the Calvinists of Geneva, that " their religion consists in attacking that of others."

But, you'll say, I know Protestants who believe in JESUS CHRIST, or hold other truths with a belief which seems well defined and precise. You must allow that such, at least, have religion. Not at all. They have some convictions, or, as they are more generally designated, some *persuasions;* all which is very good, and we praise the Lord for it. But it is not Protestantism that gives them those personal convictions, those individual persuasions. They may throw them aside to-morrow, and still not cease being Protestants. Not a few ministers glory in their name of Protestants, and still do not believe in any of the dogmas held by Luther or Calvin, and ridicule the Bible and the divinity of Jesus Christ, at the same time making a great noise about Christianity and pure Gospel.

The parson. Vinet candidly acknowledges, with a great many more concessions of the same kind, that Protestantism is not a religion, but *the bond of a religion.* (Le lien d'une religion. *Essai sur la manifestation des convictions religieuses.*)

It is well known how the celebrated Bayle, a Protestant by birth, and an infidel in practice, made reply to a distinguished personage who had questioned him about his belief. "You are a Protestant, Monsieur Bayle, but of what sect? Are you Lutheran, Calvinist, Zwinglian, or Anabaptist?" "I am none of all these," answered the consistent Protestant; "I am a Protestant, which means, I *protest* against all sorts of religion."

Protestantism, in spite of its pretensions, is not and cannot be a religion, much less is it the true religion.

XVI. DOES PROTESTANTISM BELIEVE IN JESUS CHRIST? — Thank God there are yet Protestants, honest and religious, who believe in JESUS CHRIST. But is it because they are Protestants that they believe in him? Not at all. You can be a Protestant, a genuine one, ay more, a Protestant pastor of souls, without being in the least obliged to believe in the divinity of the Redeemer. The pastor Coquerel, of Paris, has just published a thick volume (*La Christologie*), for the purpose of developing this doctrine. It has been a general belief, for the last eighteen hundred years, that to be a *Christian* it was necessary to believe that Christ was the *incarnate* GOD. According to M. Coquerel, this is a mistake. It matters very little whether JESUS be God, or some supernatural being, or a common man. Why bother one's head about it? After all, one can be a very good Christian without making so many distinctions.

Mr. T. Colani, the learned editor of the "Protestant Theological Review," published in Strasbourg, takes particular pains not to contradict his brother of Paris, and teaches his pupils, who are trained to be ministers of the Gospel, that one can indeed be a Christian without believing in JESUS CHRIST, and then he unctuously adds, "that were both JESUS CHRIST and his sanctity taken from us, it would be a great calamity for the world; but there would still remain faith,—faith in the Father, faith in GOD." (*Revue de Theologie*, Vol. vii., p. 242.)

Thus M. de Gasparin, an ardent champion of French Protestantism, congratulates himself on a triumph, as it were unexpected, that of *seven hundred* ministers *two hundred* at least believed in the divinity of Christ. (*Intérêts generaux du Protestantism*, p. vii.)

It has been proclaimed, from the most illustrious pulpits of the Reformation, that " the Saviour was only a *Jewish Socrates*, the author of the best practical philosophy."

According to some of the most celebrated ministers, he was " a *simple Rabbi*, but so many of the people persisted in believing that he was the Messiah, that at last he believed it himself; still he taught only a *pure Mosaism*, and he was condemned to death, and nailed to a cross, and laid out *having the appearance of a dead man*, and came to life again after the third day, and lastly, after having revisited his disciples on different occasions, he abandoned them without seeing them any more."

Nor is it in the writings of Voltaire or Rousseau that I find this infamous parody of the symbol of the Apostles; I read it in the *Christian Theology* of Wegscheider (*Theol. Chr. Dogm.* § 121), which has gone through seven or eight editions, and has been adopted as the text-book for those who aspire to the ministry.

It is no wonder, then, that Mr. Leblois, a minister of Strasbourg, being formed after those principles, should have, on the 31st day of December, A. D. 1854, publicly maintained from his pulpit, that the worship of JESUS CHRIST is a *superstition*, severely denouncing the Protestant sects that have retained this *remnant of Popery*, and protesting that we must put a stop to this *idolatry, so repugnant to both reason and Gospel*.

Some years ago, the King of Prussia, who is both head and doctor of the Prussian Church, expressed uneasiness about the orthodoxy of the ministers and professors of his faculty of divinity in Berlin; whereupon the Dean indignantly protested in the name of his colleagues, and solemnly declared that all, none excepted, believed . . . *that Jesus had really existed.* It was an effort, an exertion for which we must really compliment the theologians of Berlin. For, their brethren in Germany *protest* not only against the divinity of Christ, but even against the reality of his person and of his existence. Such, at least, are the logical deductions from the assumptions of Strauss, whilom professor of Protestant divinity in Zurich, who is the leader of a numerous school in Germany. And all these gentlemen call themselves Christians, and after the example of Luther, Calvin & Co.; less bold, however, they palm themselves off as the reformers of Christianity.

It is long since the *Venerable Company of*

Pastors — for, thus they style themselves — assembled in Geneva, formally forbade their preachers, by a regulation of the 3d of May, 1817, to speak from the pulpit about the divinity of Christ. The few old fogies, who still persisted in this belief so incompatible with the principle of free examination, were obliged to separate themselves, and are to this day sneered at by the National Church, and nick-named *Mômiers*.

Were it not that my limits are narrow, I might here pass in review the different Protesttant countries, and prove, from public and universal facts, how Luther's reformation abandons everywhere and denies the sacred and essential dogma of the divinity of JESUS CHRIST, — a dogma without which Christianity cannot exist. However, what we have quoted is more than sufficient to warrant our asserting, in the words of the unfortunate M. de Gasparin, "*The majority of Protestants are not Christians!*"

The dogma of the divinity of JESUS CHRIST, as well as all Christian teachings, are handed down to us by the Church, the living and infallible depositary of the authority of GOD.

I do not hereby mean to say that the Holy Scriptures do not prove to us the divinity of the Saviour in the clearest terms. But I merely assert that the Scriptures themselves deriving all their divine authority from the infallible teaching of the Church, whoever rejects the Church must needs lose at once the foundation of his faith in Christ.

The Protestants have discarded this authority, — hence they have no more any sure guidance in their belief, and thus, for the last three hundred years, their dogmas have dropped off one after another. They will end, if they are consistent, in framing, after a well-known Protestant, their formula of faith, thus: I BELIEVE IN NOTHING.

After having rejected the Church, Protestantism rejects JESUS CHRIST; after having rejected JESUS CHRIST, it must reject GOD himself, and thus it will have accomplished its work!

This impious work has been already consummated in a large portion of Germany. There exists a powerful and widely-spread association, *The Protestant Friends*, who recognize for their leaders the three ministers Uhlich, Wislicénius, and Sachse. These three men have obtained the adhesion of a vast number of German pastors; and the pastors of Berlin, with whom those of France so closely fraternize, have very often rendered the homage of sympathy to those *Protestant Friends*. Now, here is Uhlich's profession of faith, and his public catechism:—

"Our belief is to have none."

"The being which is called GOD is only a fictitious one."

"The true object of our veneration is ourselves."

The Protestantism dominant in northern Germany, and above all in Prussia, consists in this bold Atheism. It is the legitimate deduction from genuine Protestantism. It cannot exist but on condition of giving to human thought a perfect freedom, or rather an unlimited license. It is that or nothing.*

XVII. COULD A PROTESTANT EVER TELL WHAT AND WHY HE BELIEVETH?

Never! The reason thereof is very simple. *To believe, is to submit one's mind to the teachings of a personal authority, totally independent of the will of him who submits himself, and having a claim to such submission.* Now, where is this authority binding the Protestant to be found? In the Bible? But on the admission

---

* These heart-rending details are drawn from the interesting account of Eugene Rondu, head of the department of the Minister of Public Instruction, on the state of Protestantism in Prussia.

of most considerate Protestants, you have a right to interpret the Bible after your own views. The consistent Protestant, acting on the principle of free examination, *believeth* not, hath no *faith*. He substitutes his own reason for faith; for the divine authority of the church he substitutes the views or vagaries of the human mind.

The Protestant who, in spite of his separation from the Church, still preserves a certain Christian belief, is like a deserter, who, after his fleeing from the army, still carries with him part of his arms and uniform. He rests his belief on no support whatever. I defy him to give his reasons for it in a serious discussion, I will not say before a Catholic, but before an Infidel.

On the other hand, there is nothing more logical and more justifiable than the faith of the Catholic. The Catholic is united to JESUS CHRIST, the author of his faith, through the bonds of Holy Church, the living and permanent institution established for that very purpose by the Saviour himself, and connected with him by bonds existing for ages. The Protestant has severed this divine bond; and therefore he is separated from Jesus Christ although he may believe in him. It is not enough to call Jesus Lord and Saviour in order to partake of his kingdom: it is necessary to comply with his divine will, as he himself expressly declares.

I shall not stop here to show that a Protestant cannot rest his belief on the authority and teachings of the pastors of his sect. It is well known that it is one of the principles of Protestantism, that *all Christians are equal, and it does not behoove any one to play the teacher.* In the language of the Protestant Jean Jacques Rousseau, "Ministers do not know what they believe, nor what they aim at, nor what they say. It cannot even be ascertained what they pretend to believe." (*Lettres sur la Montagne.*)

As a comment on these words we add those of De Maistre:—

"As one of these preachers attempts to speak, on what does he rest his assertions, and *what means has he to know* that the people below are not laughing at him in their sleeves? It seems to me as if every one of his hearers says to him with a sceptical smile: 'Truly I believe that he believes I believe him!'"

XVIII. CHRISTIANITY AND CATHOLICITY ARE ONE AND THE SAME THING.— When you say Christianity you mean Catholicity; Catholicity is not an accidental form, but indeed the only one divinely instituted form of Christian religion.

From the very first ages, the Church of JESUS CHRIST has been called not only Christian, but also Catholic, in order to distinguish it from the different heresies which cut loose from her, and still persisted in calling themselves Christian, because they happened to preserve some shreds of truth.

It was our Lord JESUS CHRIST, who established upon earth this spiritual government, this religious and universal monarchy, which unites the Christians all over the world in ONE Society, ONE Church, ONE Body, which is called the CATHOLIC CHURCH. It is JESUS CHRIST himself who has established in this Church the Papacy, the Episcopate, and, as an auxiliary to Papacy and Episcopate, the Priesthood. The Pope, successor of Saint Peter, is, by *right divine*, Sovereign Pontiff of the Christian religion, the Pastor of all bishops, of all priests, and of all the faithful, the Supreme Judge of all religious questions, and the Doctor of true faith.

"There is only one way to be a Christian, and that is to be a Catholic," says Bossuet: which means to belong not only in sympathy and belief, but also in avowed and public practice, to the Catholic Church, to the Church governed by the Pope, to the only true Fold of Jesus Christ.

There has never been nor can there be but one Christianity. If Protestanism were Christianity, Catholicity could not be it.

This is not a question of form, it is one of nature. The institution of Jesus Christ cannot be made subject to the caprice of man, and the Protestant who fangles a Christianism to suit his own fancy has not the true Christianity, that Christianity which our Lord has brought into the world, and whose deposit and diffusion he has trusted to the Church.

In our times this glorious name of *Christian* has been strangely abused. From the Protestant who admits or rejects at will the divinity of Jesus Christ, to the Socialist, who sees no hope of *liberty* but in the annihilation of the Church, the whole crowd of heretics and revolutionists make a parade of their Christianity — but oh, what a Christianity!

To be a Christian is to be a Catholic: outside of Catholicity you may be a Lutheran, a Calvinist, a Mahommedan, a Mormon, a Free Thinker, a Buddhist, but you are not, you cannot be a Christian.

XIX. Protestantism and Primitive Chris-

TIANITY. — It is very common for certain Protestant sects to pretend that they have revived primitive Christianity, or rather that they are the Christianity of *Primitive Times.* Some Protestant authors have endeavored to give a color of truth to these pretensions of antiquity by forging, with great trouble, interminable genealogies, and pointing with a zeal, worthy of a better cause, to all the characteristics of the primitive Church in the different branches of the reformation. Let them do their best to cover with dust this Protestantism, which did not exist three hundred years ago; let them cover it with cobwebs like those bottles which merchants place on the front of their shops, but which, on being broken, reveal only sloe-wine and vinegar.

But such boasts are not believed, and many Protestant writers, well instructed and conscientious, avow their absurdity. However, it is not in behalf of the Catholic Church that they strip the Protestant sects of their pretensions. They do not recognize our practices of piety and the forms of our worship in the Gospel or in the writings of the Apostles: hence they accuse the Catholic Church as having encumbered Christianity with dogmas and practices which have disfigured it; and in their opinion Catholicity is as different from the Christianity of the primitive ages as the Protestantism of to-day.* This is the place to give a distinct and true idea of this Catholic Church, which is so contradictorily accused both of inactivity and stagnation, and of restlessness and innovation.

There never was, nor can there ever be, but one Church of Christ,— a Church immutable like her head and founder, who is God. But this Church is a living body, and however perfect she is from her origin, she develops and adapts her beneficial influences apace with the progress of centuries. Man does not possess at his birth that fulness of strength, that beauty of symmetry, that expansion of all his faculties, which add so much to the perfection of his nature. At his birth he possesses all this; but he has had no opportunity as yet to work out its development. But still he is always the same individual, whether he is a tender infant, an adolescent, or a full-grown man. Thus the Church, which was born with the Twelve Men in the cenacle, has grown and developed her strength through the growth of succeeding ages. Like a splendid drapery, which slowly deploys and progressively unfolds its beautiful colors, so the

* See M. DE GASPARIN, *les Ecoles du doute et l'ecole de la foi.*

Church has successively opened to the world the treasures of her doctrine and the sanctification which emanates from her bosom.

The Catholic Church is ever old and new. She teaches to-day what she taught in her primitive days. Some of her teachings have been more clearly defined, according as they have been attacked by her enemies, or the wants of the people have required more explicit definitions.

At the same time, whoever has seriously applied himself to the study of antiquity, the origin of Christianity, and the writings of the Fathers, has invariably found in the documents of ancient times repeated proofs of the perfect unity of Christian faith and religion, from the Apostolic Fathers down to our own times. The Papacy, Catholic Hierarchy, the Priesthood, the Sacrifice of Mass, and the Real Presence, Confession, the veneration of Our Lady, of saints and of relics, the prayers for the dead; in a word, whatever is attacked in our belief by dissenters, all is fully proven and justified by those monuments so venerable and so authentic.

The discoveries made, during the last twenty years, in the catacombs of Rome,* bring to

---

* The catacombs are subterraneous galleries tunnelled by the

light every day new testimonials of our faith and practices. Learned Protestants, on visiting the capital of the Christian world, admit at once the undeniable authenticity and the religious importance of these discoveries. Inscriptions, paintings, monuments, etc., etc., portray the forms of our worship, and trace the origin of our belief. The catacombs contain numerous chapels, with altars, upon which the relics of the martyrs are enshrined. On their walls frescos, greatly injured by the hand of time, still reveal the faith of the primitive Christian in the Real Presence, in the eucharistical sacrifice, and in confession. At every step you meet with proofs of the belief in the Papacy, the Episcopacy, and the Priesthood.

I happened once to visit the catacombs with a young Protestant gentleman, who had just come from Strasburg, where he had been studying for the ministry. He was greatly astonished with what he saw. He was a well-disposed young man, intelligent, and loyal. He did not dare to deny the evidence of what he saw before him, and knew not what to say.

Christians of the three first ages of the Church under the outskirts of the city of Rome, to be used both as cemeteries and an asylum during the persecutions. Many conversions are occasioned by visits to the catacombs.

I have not seen him since. God grant that those mighty truths, so plainly spoken to his heart from the walls of the catacombs, may lead him to the pale of Catholic Unity!

* XX. WHY DOES THE CATHOLIC CHURCH SPEAK LATIN? — Because she is *apostolic;* because she never varies her doctrine; because she is one and catholic.

1. The Church is *apostolic.* She is the Church of St. Peter and of the Apostles, and she has guarded with tenderness all the precious memories of the Apostles. When they parted for their mission over the four quarters of the globe, to announce to all nations the Gospel of Salvation, they found that two languages were spoken and understood by the two great divisions of mankind, — the Latin in the West and the Greek in the East. Hence they preached the Faith in Latin and Greek; their teachings and their constitutions were written in those two fine languages; and the Church has preserved these monuments with a religious veneration. This is the reason why her language in the West is Latin, and Greek in the East. Yet that, which in fact is a testimony in favor of the Church, is made the theme of reproach to her.

2. Providence had already disposed everything in advance. Latin and Greek became *dead languages*, and hence invariable; whereby they became wonderfully adapted to formulate the doctrines of the Church, which knows no variation, because she is divine. An interesting calculation, instituted on the changes of living languages, has shown that had the Church, instead of adhering to the Latin of St. Peter, St. Paul, and St. Mark, etc., adopted the French, she would have been obliged to modify the formula of the sacrament of Baptism *one hundred and sixty* times; otherwise this formula would never have expressed in the correct language the idea it must convey. By this we can form an idea of the transformations which the *Credo* should have undergone, to say nothing of the decrees of primitive councils and of ancient Popes!

3. The Church speaks Latin, not only because she is unchangeable, but because she is catholic, which means universal, and has to address herself to all times, nations, and countries. During the three or four first centuries the Latin was the language of the civilized world, and, although a vernacular language, it had that *catholic*, i. e. *universal* character which is indispensable to the language of the Church.

Whilst the world was divided into many nationalities, the Church still preserved her beautiful primitive language, and thus remained *one* in her forms as she has ever been in her essence.

Thus the Church speaks Latin because, first, she is apostolic; second, she is unchangeable; third, she is catholic.

But, it is objected, Saint Paul directs that in all Christian assemblies a language should be used which is understood by all the faithful. True, he says that much in his Epistle to the Corinthians. But the Protestants draw hence an objection which has nothing at all to do with the present question. The Apostle confines himself to the preaching, exhorting, and instructing the assembled faithful, which all, he says, must be done in the vernacular language. The word *prophecy* comprehends instructions, the speaking on things divine. The Catholic Church has invariably followed this apostolic command to the letter. Her bishops, priests, missionaries, and catechists always employ a language common to all, understood by all. They speak in the most obscure and poorest *dialects* in order that the Word of God may reach all understandings. The Protestant sects have good reason indeed to speak in vernacular and modern tongues. Languages of different geniuses, essentially variable, and forever changing, admirably express doctrines of such fluctuating characters.

XXI. THE SIMPLICITY OF PROTESTANT WORSHIP. — Simplicity is a good thing, indeed, when kept within certain limits. However, Protestant worship cannot, by any means, be called *simple;* it is hollow and naked.

Have you ever entered a Protestant temple? Oftentimes, it is one of those ancient churches which have been raised to the honor of the good GOD, and it is harrowing to see what the cold and narrow-minded heresy of Calvin has made of them. When a king falls, his palace becomes a house of no more significance than that of any citizen, and his throne a common chair. By expelling from churches usurped from us the King of kings, who deigned to dwell therein, the Protestants have desecrated them. They have razed the altars on which the Divine Sacrifice was offered. The images of the Blessed Virgin, as well as of patron saints, have been taken away. The confessionals, wherein innocence was preserved, and peace restored to the Christian, have been burnt, and four walls, a few benches, a chair, and a desk, behold all that is necessary to pay homage to the Creator of heaven and earth!

In the words of the Protestant Clausen, "Catholics consecrate the most wonderful productions of art to the ornament of churches, while Protestants shut themselves up within a temple devoid of all sorts of ornaments. This, however, does not prevent them from lavishing immense sums to ornament with decorations of art their private residences. Church music is looked upon by Catholics as a wholesome part of their religious solemnities; in Protestant countries music is made to resound everywhere but in churches."

The fact is, Protestants know full well what comfort is. They love and procure for their houses all that is comfortable and sumptuous; but naught for the house of the Lord.* It behoves, they say, that the utmost *simplicity* should characterize temples and all acts of religion. But it would be even more *simple* to dispense with temple and worship. To sleep, to drink, to eat, to attend to one's business, to live and die without being bothered by anything whatever, would it not be the perfection of *simplicity?*

However, we should not be surprised at this

---

* Unless it be the comfort of softly cushioned seats.

distressing and chilling nakedness of Protestant worship. Their temples are not sacred edifices, but only places of reunion. They even assemble, when they find it more convenient, either in a Casino, as in Geneva, or in a Theatre, as in New York, or in an Academy of Music, as in Boston; it is all the same to them. Should they take off their hats in entering the building, that is only from a habit of politeness, but not from any respect for the walls or benches.

Pastors wear no kind of sacerdotal vestments, and why should they? They are no priests, nothing must distinguish them from their co-religionists, and in fact the garment some of them throw over their black frocks appears to be greatly in contradiction with their principles.

We Catholics know very well that God has no need of pomp in his worship, and that it is only a want of our own heart. We know this well. But God had no need either of the magnificence of Solomon's Temple; he did not need the gold, incense, and myrrh, which was offered to him in the grotto of Bethlehem; but who would dare to affirm that those tokens of reverence and love were displeasing to him?

The majesty of worship raises our souls to God through the means of sacred ceremonies, and rivets on prayer the imagination which is so fleety and quick in wandering away. We are composed of soul and body, and our whole being must contribute to give glory to the Lord; our soul offers reverence, adoration, and love; but our senses contribute their part by the religious employment in which we occupy them in our churches, — an employment which both purifies and sanctifies them.

Divine worship is the expression of faith. The warmer faith is, the more splendid is the worship; according as faith is poor, the worship is naked. "Thus," says the Protestant writer quoted above, "the outward nakedness of non-Catholic Churches is truly in harmony with the state of the soul of the worshippers."

Leibnitz, a Protestant philosopher, writes that "he was not one of those, who, taking in no consideration human weakness, reject from divine worship whatever teaches the senses, under pretence that adoration is to be exhibited in spirit and truth." (*Système Theologique*, p. 107.)

Pustcuchen-Glanzow, another Protestant, adds: "In our temples, by dint of continually repeating that GOD must be adored *in spirit and in truth*, truth and spirit have disappeared altogether."

XXII. How Protestant Propagandism is neither legitimate nor logical.

When the Catholic Church, through her Bishops and Priests, points Protestant propagandism to Christians as an unjust and hateful aggression, non-Catholic journals, and the organs of revolution and rationalism bristle up and bitterly denounce the Church as having two weights and two measures, by despotically forbidding to others what she has not ceased to practise from her beginning. Such recriminations deserve an answer; and it is very simple.

All Protestant sects acknowledge that salvation can be attained in the Catholic Church. On the other hand, the Catholic Church has unceasingly protested that she is the only true Church, and that it is necessary to belong to her in order to be a child of God.

Protestants, therefore, are in open contradiction with their principles when they endeavor to wrest souls from the Catholic Church. And the Catholic Church would act in flagrant opposition to her own principles, were she not to exert her whole power and energy in bringing back to Jesus Christ those who have unfortunately been led out of her fold.

The Catholic Church, in her efforts to enlighten a Protestant and to bring him back to the true faith, preserves to him the possession of all the truth he possesses, and bestows upon him all that in which he is found wanting. It is a poor man, only half dressed, that she is endeavoring to clothe; what she adds to the little he already possesses makes a perfect Christian.

But not so when the Protestant propagandist succeeds in seducing a Catholic. It only ends by taking away from him a part of his belief and giving him nothing at all in return. He leaves him half naked, like the unfortunate traveller whom the highwayman robs of his garments, under the heartless pretence of freeing him of all unnecessary incumbrance, and without bestowing on him so much as one rag for protection against cold.

However, it is acknowledged even by Protestants, that in point of religious truths, they cannot bestow on Catholics aught that the latter do not already possess; and still farther, they aver that whatever they preserve of Christianity, it is all borrowed of the Catholic Church.

It is worth while to hear Luther, the ardent patriarch of the Reformation, on this subject. At the meeting of Marburg, when the famous dispute between Luther and Zwinglius took place, the former maintaining the dogma of the

Holy Eucharist against all adversaries, Zwinglius objected to the dogma of the Real Presence as a remnant of *Popery.*

"Well, then," quoth Luther, "reject also the holy Bible, *because it is from the Pope we have received it.* We are forced to acknowledge, Protestants as we are, that in Popery there are truths of salvation, yes, ALL the truths of salvation, and that we receive them from Popery; for it is in Popery that we find the *true Holy Scriptures, true Baptism, the true Sacrament of the altar, the true keys which pardon sin, true preaching, true catechism, the true articles of faith; and, moreover, I say, that in Popery* TRUE CHRISTIANITY is to be found." *

To acknowledge that the Catholic Church is the *true Christianity* necessarily involves the consequence that the Protestant sects have *not* the

---

* It may not be amiss to give the original text of this remarkable confession: "Hoc enim pacto negare oporteret totam Scripturam Sacram et prædicandi officium: HOC ENIM TOTUM A PAPA HABEMUS. Nos autem fatemur sub Papatu plurimum esse boni Christianismi, *imo* OMNE *bonum Christianismum,* atque etiam illinc ad nos devenisse. Quippe fatemur in Papatu veram esse Scripturam Sacram, verum Baptisma, verum Sacramentum altaris, veras claves ad remissionem peccatorum, verum prædicandi officium, verum catechismum ut sunt; Oratio Dominica, articuli fidei, decem præcepta. . . DICO INSUPER IN PAPATU VERUM CHRISTIANISMUM ESSE."—See the Protestant edition of Luther's works, published in Jena, pp. 408 and 9.

true Christianity, because the Church affirms all that the sects deny. But at the same time we must conclude, as a self-evident truth, that propagandism becomes a duty on the part of the Church, while on the part of Protestants it is merely nonsense, injustice, and an usurpation.

XXIII. A CONVENIENT RELIGION. — It is more convenient, they say, to be a Protestant, than a Catholic; and true it is, — just as true as it is a great deal easier to yield to one's passions than to restrain them. But the difference is that in point of religion we must not look for that which is the easiest, but for that which is true, and will lead to GOD.

A certain parson once gained over to his sect a good woman, who had allowed herself to be influenced by his *assertions*. She was very assiduous at the meeting-house; most regularly did she take her little siesta during the sermon on Sunday, took great care of the ponderous Bible she had received, and never opened it, lest she should spoil it, — in a word, she gave evident proofs that she had become a good Protestant. Her religious fervor urged her also to become a member of the famous *Protestant Pence*, and of two or three Bible societies.

The good woman spent several years in this

easy piety, and she congratulated herself every day on her good luck of enjoying such sweet life, which her pastor assured her was the *pure Gospel*, free from the unpleasant duty of going to confession on the recurrence of great festivals, receiving communion with certain very particular preparations, *abstaining* on Fridays, and of being obedient to her parish priest. In the midst of all this *evangelical* happiness, which was enhanced by the little presents and various tracts she received from the minister and some deaconess, the poor creature was all at once taken down by sickness. A *reader* was appointed to visit her, and read psalms and other passages, of which she understood very little; in fact, no more than the zealous *reader* himself. She grew worse, and her physician let out expressions which were very far from warranting her recovery. In the presence of death, and at the approach of the judgment of God, the poor woman shuddered, and seriously thought of her chances. In that light which does not deceive, she began to feel that she had gone astray from *the* Faith. She begged of a neighbor to bring to her, without delay, the priest of the parish, a good and worthy clergyman whom she had known long ago, and whom her apostasy had grieved to the heart. He found her in tears, consoled her as well as he could, and made her both aware of the enormity of her sin, and confident in the infinite mercy of God. She made her confession, and was reconciled with our Saviour. Then he administered to her Extreme Unction, the Sacrament that brings so much comfort to the dying, which she had lately been taught to laugh at, but the importance and efficacy whereof she at this moment understood well. Lastly, he carried to her the holy Viaticum, that most holy and most adorable mystery, within which Jesus Christ veils himself, in order that we may approach, and he may fortify us at the end of our journey. Having made her peace with God and with her soul, the poor woman felt happy, and already looked without fear to the moment of her entering into eternity.

On the evening of the same day, the Protestant minister calls on the sick woman. He had just heard of the priest's visit, and he could not believe what he called " a scandalous defection, a shame to the pure Gospel, a falling back upon the superstitions of Babylon." In fact, what vexed him most was the talk of the neighborhood, as inferences would be made in disparagement of the *pure Gospel*, and hurtful to the susceptibilities of the reverend pastor.

Accordingly he expostulated in strong terms with the sick woman, reminding her of the courage with which she had before rejected "all such mummeries," and those errors which she ought to have never again adopted. "Ah! sir," replied the good woman, "all this was very good when I was well; *your religion is a very easy one to live in, but very hard to die in!* (*C'est bien commode pour vivre, mais c'est le diable pour mourir !*)

She felt, the brave woman, that with that simple expression she had placed her finger on the sore spot of Protestantism.

Now, a system of religion, which only aims at being easy in practice, and discards whatever may prove irksome in the service of GOD, cannot be the true religion, — the religion that leads to heaven. Protestantism is very convenient to live in; hence it is so horrible to die in it. Protestantism is easy, and hence it is false, — it is not the religion of him who said: "*How narrow is the gate, and strait is the way that leadeth to life!*" from which words we have to conclude that *we must then struggle to enter that gate and to strike upon that way.*

Protestantism, a pretended Christianity, without obedience to faith, without obedience to the authority of the Church, without confession, without eucharist, without sacrifice, without works of penance, without practices of obligation, is condemned by that Gospel whose name it so often usurps; and is it not condemned by JESUS CHRIST, when the divine Master adds those terrible words: "*Wide is the gate and broad is the way that leadeth to destruction*"?

XXIV. A TOUCHSTONE. — It is easy to distinguish the true religion from those which are pretentious of being called true.

Our Lord has solemnly declared that his disciples shall be hated by the wicked as he had been hated himself: "*The disciple is not above his Master; if the world hate you, know ye that it hath hated me before you.*" (John xv. 18.)

Now, history teaches us that from the days of the apostles, the hatred and the efforts of the impious have always been combined against the Catholic Church. Jews, and Pagans, and Turks, and the wicked of all ages, and of our own times, have always taken for the butt, and the only butt of their attacks, the Catholic Church, — the Catholic Church alone. During the French Revolution brigands have always aimed their first blows at her: they imprisoned and butchered her bishops and priests, and at the same time they left Jewish rabbis and Protestant ministers alone. Read the bloody proclamations of our modern revolutionists. ONLY the Catholic Church awakens all their fury. Nor do they only abstain from annoying Protestantism, but they moreover exalt it as highly favorable to their anti-Christian views.

This coalition of the wicked against the Catholic Church is already an evident realization of the prophecy of our Lord. An additional proof has been afforded by the heretical sects, and above all, the Protestant ones. Separated from one another, opposed to each other in views and interests, condemning one another, they will uniformly act in a most harmonious alliance when there is question of injuring or attacking St. Peter's old Church. In the face of this common enemy, they become one, and they blaspheme in unison.

Herod and Pilate, whilom enemies, became united to crucify JESUS. Heresy and impiety, separated as they may be, become united for the purpose of outraging, scourging, and annoying the holy Church of Christ.

However, if the Church, catholic, apostolic, and Roman, must needs, in imitation of her founder, endure her own *passion*, and thus com-

plete that of her Chief, she possesses equally with <u>him</u> the promises of life eternal. Ever hated, ever blasphemed, she lives, and will live forever. JESUS is with her, unto the end of the world, and to her alone he has said: "The powers of hell shall not prevail against thee."

PART SECOND.

I. Can the Church ever need Reformation?—Dear reader, however strong and healthy you are, you may occasionally be subject to some derangement, which, not the least affecting the soundness of your constitution, will make it necessary that you should purify your blood, and have recourse to some medicine. That these remedies may attain their desired effect, they must be administered with knowledge and prudence. Place yourself in the hand of doctors established for this purpose, and have no recourse to charlatans or quacks, who will endanger your health and perhaps send you to the graveyard.

Thus the Church also, divine though she be, may need reforms. The Church is the society of the disciples of Jesus Christ. He has promised to be with his Church unto the end of the world, to preserve in her true faith, and true morality. By the assistance of Our Lord the Church is therefore *infallible* and *holy*.

But the Church is composed of men. Popes, bishops, and priests are men. In spite of the intrinsic sanctity of their ministry, they are subject to the imperfections and weakness of human nature. We can then well understand in what sense the Church has needed and will always need reforms. There will never be any need of rectifying the teachings of her faith, divine as it is and infallible. She will never need to reform her morality, which is holy, nor change her sacraments, through which she sanctifies man. But she constantly needs to recall to a sense of their duty those among her children, and even her ministers, who, being but fallible, may prevaricate or disregard the observance of her laws.

For eighteen hundred years Popes and Councils and Synods have indefatigably labored to reform what may become relaxed from time to time in matters of discipline. Such was eminently the work of the Council of Trent, which has *definitely* reformed the Church.

It was a great mistake of Luther and his associates to mix up, in this question, the essence with the form, what is divine and unchangeable with what is human and susceptible of changes. They have taken into their heads to reform the dogma, the rule of faith, and the principles of morality. Instead of a true *reformation* they have only begotten a disastrous rebellion, which has deformed and upset everything.

They were quacks, no physicians. Under pretext of drawing a decayed tooth they have broken the jaw. Instead of purging the system they have poisoned it.

II. CAN GOD HAVE CHOSEN LUTHER AND CALVIN TO REFORM RELIGION?—GOD is holy. Accordingly he could never have chosen Luther, Calvin, Henry VIII., or the like of them, for the purpose of reforming the Church.

The Protestant historian Cobbett remarks, that "Luther, Zwinglius, Calvin, etc., agreed on only one point of doctrine, and that was that all *good works are useless*, and certainly their lives prove that they followed the principle in earnest." (Hist. Ref. Prot., vii. 200.)

What was Luther, in spite of his popular eloquence and the powerful temper of his mind, but a *bad priest?* and can there be anything more disgraceful?

Calvin was also an ecclesiastic. Convicted

of infamous crimes against nature, he was publicly branded by the executioner.*

Zwinglius, a curate of Einsiedlen, publicly avowed, in the presence of his bishop, that he had for many years yielded to his lust, and would now marry a woman in order to render his position lawful before the people.

All the *saints* of the reformation are of this stamp. The *spotless* purity and *evangelical* meekness of Henry VIII. is well known; and he is the reformer of England! That sensualist a veritable Bluebeard, had six wives whose heads he cut off accordingly as he became tired of them. His daughter, Elizabeth, the *virgin* queen, carried out the work commenced by Henry VIII., and was no less renowned for the same fine qualities. The same block could receive the heads of the mistresses of the father as well as those of the paramours of the daughter.

But Calvin deserves a little more notice. It is he who introduced Protestantism into France. Galiffe, a Protestant Calvinist, has portrayed

* This is an historical fact. These shameful stigmas of the patriarch of Calvinism having been cast up to them by a Catholic writer, Whitacker had the sacrilegious effrontery of replying that "if Calvin was *marked*, so St. Paul and many others have been."

him, better than any one else, in his *Notices Genealogiques* (t. iii. pp. 21 etc.), published in the very heart of Geneva in 1836 : "That name, famous for its criminality, raised the standard of the most ferocious intolerance, of the grossest superstitions, and most impious tenets. A terrible apostle, from whose inquisition nothing escaped. During 1558 and 1559 he caused one hundred and fourteen judgments to be given in criminal matters," etc. Mr. Galiffe styles him a *drinker of blood*, and supports all his assertions by the writings of Calvin himself, and by proofs drawn from the public and authentic archives of Geneva.

As for Luther, he was an apostate monk, living in concubinage with an unfrocked nun, and he has been judged by Protestant writers with merited severity. His life, after his apostasy, was that of a libertine entirely taken with the pleasures of the table, and animal pleasures, so much so that it had become a proverb, in occasions of self-indulgence, to say: To-day we shall live *à la Luther*. Benedict Morgenstern, a Protestant writer, records this fact.*
The *Table Talk* of Luther can be still found in

---

* *Traité de l'Eglise*, p. 21. "Si quando volunt indulgere genio, non vereantur inter se dicere: *hodie lutheranice vivemus.*"

some libraries shelved among obscene books; it breathes such a cynicism, that it is impossible to quote from them. Every one knows that ignoble prayer, written in Luther's own hand, the authenticity whereof has never been disputed, and whose conclusion runs thus: "Good drinking and good eating; behold the surest means of being happy."

And they would make us believe, that men of this stamp were messengers sent by Our Lord JESUS CHRIST to the Christians charged with the mission of bringing the Church back to its primitive purity! — Nonsense! You might then as well believe, with the Turks, that "GOD is GOD and Mahommed is his prophet!" Good sense ought to prevail over the historical falsehoods by which they have endeavored to rehabilitate those pretended reformers.

The founder of the Catholic Church is our Lord JESUS CHRIST, and her apostles are Saint Peter, and Saint Paul, Saint John, and the other messengers of Faith appointed by the Founder.

The founder of Protestantism is Luther, and its apostles Calvin, Zwinglius, & Co.

There's a choice for you.

III. HAVE THE APOSTLES OF PROTESTANTISM ANY CREDENTIALS TO SHOW. — By two infallible marks we can ascertain whether a man who presents himself as a reformer of the Church is in reality sent by God. These two marks are holiness and the gift of miracles.

We need not speak of the sanctity of Luther and Calvin. The world knows what to think of their sanctity. The mention of such disgraceful recollections brings shame to the cheeks of candid and honest Protestants.

As for miracles, they would have liked to perform some. But it is not so easy a task as that of forming a sect. Erasmus remarks, with a sneer, "that none of them could yet heal a lame horse."

Calvin took into his head once to perform a little miracle. Unfortunately he failed. He hired a man to play the dead, that he might resuscitate him. When he came to the spot, followed by a curious crowd to whom he had innocently promised this proof of his mission, God's justice had smitten the partner of his imposture, and poor Calvin was well-nigh to die of fright, finding the wretch stiff in death. This is a fact well authenticated in history.

But Luther got out of the difficulty in another fashion. Should any one dare to ask him for some miraculous sign by which to prove that he spoke in the name of God, he replied with a torrent of abuse, and the unlucky interloper was dismissed with the qualifications of being an *ass*, a *Turk*, a *dog*, a *bedevilled hog*.

The fathers of the Reformation had neither *sanctity* nor the power of performing *miracles*. They were *not* the envoys of GOD.

What spirit has, then, inspired them with its powerful breath? The spirit of vain-glory, the spirit of impurity, the spirit of rebellion, which has never ceased to wage war against the Christ and his work: an infernal spirit which has begotten heresies, and is the veritable spirit of Protestant anarchy. *You are of your father, the devil* (St. John viii. 44).

IV. THE CHURCH EMINENTLY POSSESSES THE DIVINE PROOF. — MIRACLES are the mark which excels all others with the evidence of its light. Our Lord appealed to this mark alone to prove to his apostles and disciples, and then to his adversaries, the mysteries of his Divinity; for he said to them, "If you do not believe my words, then believe my miracles; the miracles I perform give testimony of me."

The enemies of JESUS admitted the reality of those wonders, and were enraged at the impression they made. *This man*, they said, *performs so many miracles, and the whole world goes after him!* The great miracle of the Resurrection, well ascertained by the *evidence* of the senses of seeing and touching, alone convinced the obstinate incredulity of the apostles, and especially of St. Thomas, who threw himself at the feet of the triumphant Christ only after having put his fingers into the wounds of his hands and feet, and his hand into the ever open wound of his Sacred Heart.

A *miracle*, the act superhuman and essentially divine, is, then, the greatest proof of JESUS CHRIST. It is also the great proof of his Church.

Nor does the Church incessantly perform miracles by the virtue of Christ living in his saints, but she is, moreover, a living miracle, public and never ceasing, such an one as to surpass all scientific demonstrations. It is a miracle equally intelligible to the poor and the ignorant as to the learned and the philosopher. St. Augustine, from the very early ages of faith, proclaimed loudly, that "the establishment of Christianity in the world without great miracles would be in itself the greatest and most wonderful of all miracles."

The apostles and their disciples for three or four centuries raised the dead to life, healed the sick, gave sight to the blind, hearing to the deaf, and the use of their limbs to the palsied. With only the sign of the cross they caused the idols to fall, and the temples of the gods to crumble into heaps of ruin. In spite of those ages of butchery, in spite of that fury of man which even miracles could not subdue, the Church, Catholic, Apostolic, and Roman, came forth from the catacombs, after having triumphed over human opposition.

She was then herself a great miracle, which means a work evidently superhuman attesting the almighty power of God. And thus she has progressed through all ages, carrying on her brow the divine testimony, asserting her rights even as Christ asserted his, and having no need whatsoever of further proof for herself.

The divine fact of her existence, and especially of her sovereign pontificate, assumes in every age more gigantic proportions. St. Irenæus, even at the close of the second century, quoted this durability of the Roman Church, in the midst of contradictions, as an irrefragable proof of her divine origin; but what would he say, were he to live in the nineteenth?

The Church is then a living miracle, and her very existence is, I repeat it, the great proof of her divinity. Let poor Protestant ministers write and fret as much as they please in the face of this divine fact. Like the scribes of old, in the presence of JESUS giving life to Lazarus, they are crushed by the superhuman power of this Catholic fact.

V. THE REFORMERS THEIR OWN JUDGES.— There are Protestants who still cling to the memory of their great reformers, and are jealous of whatever may concern their name and fame. Like the children of Noah, they throw a mantle over the turpitude of their fathers, and raise a cry of indignation should any one allow himself to think that Luther and Calvin were not patterns of goodness. They continually accuse Catholic writers of lying, and slandering. Luther and Calvin are to them as pure as lambs in spite of the verdict of history.

To give such charges their own weight, and to enable my readers to form a true estimate of these new apostles, I will only copy the opinions rendered by the chiefs of the Reformation on one another. As they knew each other better than any one else, these portraits will be truly after nature.

Let us begin with Luther. All hail to the chief! Hear how he is portrayed by Calvin: "Indeed Luther is very wicked. Would to

God, he had taken more pains in controlling his libertinism! Would to God he had better known how to acknowledge his vices!"

"When I read one of Luther's books," says Zwinglius (ŒUVRES II. 474), "I think I see a nasty swine grunting around and tearing up the sweet flowers of a fine garden. Luther cannot speak of God and of holy things, but with procacity, great ignorance of theology, and impropriety." Luther returns tit for tat, saying: "Zwinglius dreams to be a sun that illumines the world, but he gives no more light than dung would in a lamp . . . *stercus in lucerna.*"

Nor is Calvin less severely disposed of by his collaborers in the work of Reformation, those who should have felt most interested in palliating his faults. Volmar, his first professor, says: "Calvin is violent and perverse: so much the better, for he is the man we need to further our interests."* Bucer, an apostate monk, and a married priest, adds a touch to the limning: "Calvin in all truth is a mad dog: he is a bad man . . . Be on thy guard, O Christian reader! against Calvin's books."† But hear how Theodore Beza, Cal-

* See FREUNDELFELD. *Analytical Table of Universal History,* II. 369.
† Ibid. Scriptor maledicendi studio infectus, canis rabidus.

vin's favorite disciple, treats his master: "Calvin could never be trained either to temperance or to honest habits, or to truthfulness: he was always stuck in the mud."

Zwinglius, according to his favorite disciple Bullinger, was expelled from his parish for his immorality. In spite of his being a priest, and a parish priest, he was publicly married, after the fashion of Luther. "If you are told," says he in a letter, "that I have given in to pride, intemperance, and impurities, believe it, for it is true: I am a prey to these vices and many others."* Of him Luther declared that he was *satanized, in-satanized, over-satanized*, and that not the least hope could be entertained of his salvation.

Nor has the great Theodore de Beza, that pious individual of whom we find so many eulogies in Protestant writers, fared any better in the opinion of the most fervent partisans of the Reformation. Heshussius (transl. of Florimond, p. 1048) exclaims: "How can any one wonder at the incredible impudence of this monster, whose lewd and infamous life is so well known over all France, through his epigrams worse than cynic? And still in hearing him you would say that he was a holy man,

* Hospinien. *Hist. of the Sacraments*, II. 187.

another Job, or a modern anchorite of the desert, even a greater man than Saint John or Saint Paul, he boasts so much, on every occasion, of his exile, his labors, his purity, and the wonderful sanctity of his life!"—Schlussemberg, another writer of the same sect, remarks: "This obscene man, equal to a devil incarnate, kneaded with cunning and impiety, can do naught but belch forth satirical blasphemies..."

Shortly before he was smitten with apoplexy Luther embodied all these testimonies and added with his own hand: "In truth we are only blackguards."

But a truce to this subject. Volumes might be filled with the reproaches and recriminations which the so-called reformers have bandied with one another. On the other hand, the quotations which we have before us are of a character which we should loathe to place before the eyes of decent readers.

Let, then, the children of Luther and of his companions raise no more the cry of calumny when a Catholic voice is raised from time to time to give a judgment of their fathers and to impeach them. Never did the Church, in casting them off, brand them with expressions of such crushing force as those they have employed themselves, a small sample whereof we have just recalled to mind.

It would be more to the liking of Protestants were these revelations, so suggestive and so damning, allowed to lie forgotten or hidden. Of course, their vanity suffers by such exposures; but is it not necessary that light be made and justice rendered in the face of the never-ceasing efforts of Protestant propagandism?

VI. ON THE DIVISIONS OF PROTESTANTISM. — During eighteen hundred years, the Catholic Church, Apostolic and Roman, founded by Christ, and governed in his name by Saint Peter, and the Supreme Pontiffs his successors, has preserved the most perfect unity in the teaching of faith and in the practice of religion. From the beginning have innovators without number endeavored to introduce their individual ideas into the creed of this great Church. But she has invariably repelled them, and her doctrine, which shall last eternally, has remained one and pure.

During these last three hundred years, since the great rebellion has broken out, Protestantism has followed a course altogether different. Protestantism acknowledges as its fathers the Gnostics, the Arians, the Manicheans, the Nestorians, the Iconoclasts, the Albigenses, the Hussites, and the most scandalous of heretics. As a carcass will swarm with vermin, so this corpse of religion, dating its existence from such inglorious traditions, has never ceased down to our times to produce hundreds and myriads of sects which swarm out of its bosom. They gnaw its vitals, and gnaw one another. It is simply impossible to give the exact statistics of Protestant sects. What was accurate yesterday would not be so to-day. They spring into life and die away like flies. So far back as 1743, the Protestant minister Froereisen, in his address on being installed minister at Strasburg, acknowledged that "Protestantism is like a vermin, cut into many pieces which will move as long as there exists some strength, but will by degrees lose both life and motion."

In fact, what is a Protestant sect? Free discussion gives each and every one of its members an inalienable right to an absolute independence, so as to break the factitious unity of a body to which he is said to belong. Make up as many religions as there are sects, as many sects as there are heads, and in each head as many religious notions as there are whims, and you have a befitting idea of Protestant unity. The minister Vinet said it with grief, that "from the morrow after the Reformation, Protestants have existed, but no Protestantism."

I have before me an article clipped from an American paper giving a list, not complete however, of all the sects which existed in the State of New York. Let us copy it here:—
Anabaptists, Baptists, New Baptists, Free Baptists, Separate Baptists, Strict Baptists, Liberal Baptists, Peace Baptists, Small Children Baptists, Glory Baptists, Hallelujahs, Christian Baptists, Iron Arm Baptists, General Baptists, Particular Baptists, Seventh Day Baptists, Six Principle Baptists, Scotch Baptists, Baptists of the New Communion General, Black Baptists, the Independent or Puritans, the Cameronians, Shrivelled or Crispers, Campbellites or Reformed, Dunkers, Free Thinkers, Haldanites, Huntingdonians, Irvingites, Inghanites, Jumpers, Biblical Christians, Glassites or Sandomonians, Old Presbyterians, and New Presbyterians, Scotch Congregationalists, Quakers or Friends, Unitarians, Socinians, Moravians or Unity Friends, Methodists or Wesleyans, Primitive Methodists, Reformed Wesleyans, French Methodists, Calvinists, Original Connexionists and New Connexionists, Swedenborgians, Plymouth Brothers, Rebaptized Christians, Mormons, Kellyites, Muggletonians, Romanian Per-

fectionalists, Rogessian Methodists, Secklers, Universalists, Walkers, Rothfieldists, Free Friend Disciples or Agapemonites, Lutherans, French Protestants, Reformed Protestants, German Protestants, Reformed German Protestants, German Catholics or Followers of Ronge, New Illuminati, English Anglicans, German Anglicans, French Anglicans, etc., etc., etc." Prodigious fecundity!

Surely France is not blessed with such an abundance. For there exist only some of the Reformed sects, the Protestants of the Augsburg Confession, Methodists, Anabaptists, Baptists, Pietists, Unitarians, Latitudinarians, Darbyites, Irvingians. . . . . . It is, however, rather difficult to find out the fecundity of the varieties of French Protestantism, inasmuch as its pastors generally affect an air of touching fraternity, and take great pains to carry on their bickerings with closed doors, most carefully keeping out of sight what one of them indiscreetly calls *clerical family snarls.** They seem afraid of French good sense, which would very easily draw from their variations and divisions, the famous consequence drawn in olden times by

* *Les entre-mangeries pastorales.* Le Principes de légalité et la conscience confessionelle de certains pasteurs soi-disant Lutheriens, par J. G. Baum, p. 1.

Tertullian against Marcion: " Thou art at variance, therefore thou errest."

How majestic, on the other hand, how grand is the Catholic Church, with her hierarchy, the guardian of her unity against the intestine discords and the interminable dismemberments which take place around her!

Florimond de Rémond, in his *History of the Rise and Progress of Heresy*, remarks, in his old and quaint style: Had ye ever seen a regiment of noble soldiers with serried ranks, marching under the lead of a cuirassed chief, and after them the musketeers in beautiful order, and then the arquebusiers, with the rest of the troops, all keeping steps to the measured beat of the drum, and then had ye seen a swarm of monkeys, trotting about the streets carrying wooden swords and shouldering long reeds, beating their music on a tin pan, and every mother's son among them giving orders to his comrades, — well, ye would then recognize in the first the order of the true Church, and in the latter the disorders of those bastard churches which ape the True One.

VII. WHAT WE SHOULD THINK OF FREEDOM OF THOUGHT. — The freedom of thinking is simply nonsense. We are no more free to think without rule than we are to act without one. Unless we prefer to be disorderly and incur damnation, we are bound to have thoughts of truth and of truth alone; just as we are bound to do what is right and only what is right. Is not this evident?

Are you left at liberty to think that two and two are not four? Are you free to think that the whole is not greater than the part, that vice is not better than virtue, that Charlemagne did not exist, etc.? And why are you not left at your own liberty on these points, but because they are truths?

By this universal principle is man's understanding ruled. It must need be applied above all, and in all its force, to the most important of all truth,—religious truth. We are not free to discuss a truth; or to reject it. But the mysteries of Christian faith are truths; and such are the Catholic dogmas of the Trinity, Divine Incarnation, Original Sin, Redemption, Grace, Church, Eternity of Punishment, etc., etc. They are therefore all *charged* on our understanding, because they all are *truths*. We are sure that they are truths because GOD has revealed them through his Son JESUS CHRIST, who, in his turn, has entrusted them as a deposit and for an infallible teaching to his Church.

Freedom of thought is the soul of Protestantism; it is likewise the soul of modern rationalistic philosophy. It is one of those impossibilities which only the levity of a superficial reason can regard as admissible. But a sound mind, that does not feed on empty words, looks upon this freedom of thought only as simply absurd, and, what is more, as sinful.

It is the same with the liberty of conscience, the freedom of saying and doing whatever may please us. Freedom, forsooth! Such freedom as will lead you to perdition, if it is not controlled by the divine teaching of Christ, and of his Church.

Catholic authority does not destroy, nay, it protects and quickens human thought. It is the authority of truth. Its immutability is not the restraint which prevents a flight; it is the guard which prevents explosion or destruction. The authority of the Church is a guard over human understanding in whatever directly or indirectly affects religion, which means in every kind of doctrines, religious, philosophical, scientific, political, etc.

Only in the Church can the spirit of man, supported by authority, find the true freedom of thought.

VIII. Religious Differences among Catholics. — Occasionally Catholics are divided on a religious question. It is discussed and much is written pro or con. Impious people, who cannot understand these contests, draw conclusions unfavorable to religion itself. But are these divisions actually of so much importance as it is pretended? Have they any resemblance to those of Protestants?

Not the least. All Catholics have the same faith, because they are all animated by the one principle of faith, which is obedience to the teachings of the Church. They are all of one accord on what is dogma properly so called; while it is against this very dogma that Protestant sects always split. Their pretended meeting on a common ground, which they call *fundamental points*, is only an illusion vanishing before facts. Except on God's existence they agree in nothing else. Only a short time ago M. de Gasparin publicly averred that, of the *seven hundred* ministers, who preached Protestantism and assail the Church in France, *five hundred* did not believe in the divinity of Jesus Christ, the holy Trinity, baptismal regeneration, etc. Many, after the lead of Prof. Schoerer of Geneva, do not believe in the inspiration of the Bible. It is then precisely on *fundamental points*, and the only ones which are *fundamental*, that Protestants have become separated, as the great Bossuet demonstrated two centuries ago.

The Catholics, on the other hand, are allowed to debate only on such points of doctrine, which the Church does not propose to them as matter of faith, and are therefore qualified as *opinions*. Opinions are open to discussion, and thus they differ from belief. Hence it is that being allowed to defend their opinions, Catholic doctors, and even bishops, express and maintain their sentiments against one another. Interesting dissertations and essays are generally the result of these doctrinal struggles, and in the aggregate they enhance the value of theological science, which is not merely the catechism of faith, but even the work of the human mind built upon the unchangeable and grand foundation of faith.

Should the Church think proper, in her wisdom, to define any of these controverted doctrines, Catholics then are no more at liberty to discuss them, and they *believe*. Opinion in that case becomes a dogma, and what was heretofore debatable as doubtful will henceforward be certain.

Moreover these differences among Catholics bear mostly on the different appreciation of expedients. For instance; some deem it preferable for the good of religion that its enemies were attacked in front, no compromise allowed, and their errors met with determined energy. Others will qualify this conduct as one of violence and of imprudence; they only put a different interpretation on the principles of charity, and maintain that it is necessary to tame the wolf.

It is evident that such differences impair not our religious unity; and yet they afford a source of scandal to those good Protestant pastors who are so very fond of unity, truth, and charity! Verily they are unfortunate people who see the mote in our eye, but perceive not the beam which obstructs their own sight!

IX. How the Teaching of the Church is the true Rule of Faith. — By a *Rule of Faith* is understood that which determines what Christians have to believe, and what to reject.

Now, what is this rule to which we must conform ourselves in order to determine our belief? Where and which is the true Rule of Faith?

Here, as well as in everything else, Protestants are at variance with the Catholic Church. Fifteen hundred years after the preaching of the Apostles, Luther finds out that the whole world has been going astray. The true, the only rule of faith, quoth he, is the Bible. All Protestants admit this principle; but of it more anon. For the present let us aver what the Christians have believed from the days of the Apostles to those of Luther, what we believe ourselves after the example of our fathers, and what the Christians who will come after us will believe to the world's end.

Our Lord appointed twelve among his disciples, and sent them forth to the world, to teach in his name and with his authority the Christian religion:—

All power is given to me in heaven and in earth.

Going therefore, teach all nations whatever I have commanded you. Matt. xxviii.

Go ye unto the whole world and preach the gospel to every creature. Mark xvi.

He that heareth you heareth me; and he that despiseth you despiseth me. Luke x.

Behold, I am with you all days, even to the consummation of the world. Matt. xxviii.

By these last words the Son of GOD makes it sure, that the spiritual power and the mission of the Apostles was to be a permanent ministry, even to the consummation of the world. Now, if there exists an irrefutable historical fact, it is that, from the Apostles to this day, the pastors of the Catholic Church, ascending through a legitimate and uninterrupted precession, to Saint Peter and the other Apostles, have exercised and do exercise this ministry.

And in what does this ministry consist? That power which is derived from JESUS CHRIST himself, and by which *fallible* men teach us *infallibly*, and *infallibly* lead us in the path of salvation? It is the authority of the Church, to wit, the authority of the Sovereign Pontiff, successor of St. Peter, head of the Church, and the authority of the bishops, coadjutors to the Pope in the grand work of the salvation of men.

This divine authority, intrusted as it is to the hands of men, is the true, the only Rule of Faith. It has been thus believed in all Christian ages; it has been thus taught by all doctors and fathers of the Church. We have to believe only what the Pope and the Bishops teach. We have to reject only that which the Pope and the Bishops condemn and reject. Should a point of doctrine appear doubtful, we have only to address ourselves to the Pope and to the Bishops in order to know what to believe. Only from that tribunal, forever living and forever assisted by God, emanates the judgment on religious belief, and particularly on the true sense of the Scriptures.

Such is the Rule of Faith followed by all true Christians; it is a rule of divine institution, and no one can knowingly reject it without imperilling the salvation of his soul. *He that despiseth you despiseth me!* (Luke x.) Such is the immovable principle of unity and life in the Church. It is owing to this that Catholics have ever believed the same one thing for eighteen hundred years.

The Protestants have not this divine rule, and hence as St. Paul has it, they are *children tossed to and fro, and carried about by every wind of doctrine.* — (Eph. iii. 14.) In spite of the Bible, which they hold up so sanctimoniously, they believe to-day what they rejected yesterday, to reject again to-morrow the belief of to-day, until, through a wonderful operation of believing and disbelieving, they will end in believing nothing.

Then, it becomes necessary summarily to examine this pretension of theirs, by which the invariable and ever-living authority of the Church is displaced for a book, undoubtedly divine, but lifeless and dumb as all books are, and which can do no good where it is read in a wrong sense.

X. THE HOLY BIBLE IS NOT, NOR CAN IT BE,

THE RULE OF FAITH. — The Bible is undoubtedly the word of GOD. We Catholics know it, even better than Protestants. The Bible contains naught but what is the teaching of God. And yet the Bible is not, the Bible cannot be, the Rule of our faith, in the Protestant sense.

Why?

First. The Bible cannot be the rule of our faith, because JESUS CHRIST has not said to his disciples 'go and carry the Bible,' but he said, *Go and teach all nations — he that heareth you heareth me.* Lessing, a Protestant, remarks that "Christianity had already been diffused before any of the evangelists undertook to write the life of JESUS. They repeated the *Our Father* before St. Matthew had written the words, for JESUS CHRIST himself had taught it to his disciples, who had *transmitted* it to the primitive Christians . . . . . Baptism was administered in the name of the Father, and of the Son, and of the Holy Ghost, before St. Matthew had drawn up the formula of baptism in his Gospel, for JESUS CHRIST had *verbally* taught it to his disciples." — (Beiträge für Geschicte und Litteratur, t. iv. p. 182.)

To this proof of fact we must add another, which Protestants can never answer with even the appearance of reasoning.

passages of Holy Writ. Those words of our Saviour at the last supper, THIS IS MY BODY, have received upwards of *two hundred* interpretations at the hand of Protestants!

Fourthly and lastly. The word of GOD in the Bible is not, nor can it be, a Rule of Faith for Christians; because, if it were, then the Christian religion would not have been established for the Poor and Little ones,—that is to say, for those whom JESUS has distinguished as the privileged children of his love.

However, this last point is worth the trouble of being treated apart.

XI. PROTESTANTISM IS NOT, NOR CAN IT BE THE RELIGION OF THE PEOPLE. — No; Protestantism is not made for the people. Jesus loves the poor and the humble. But Protestantism, in giving the reading of the Bible as the fundamental rule of Christian Faith, excludes the people from Christianity. In fact, many among the poor cannot read, and what is a book for those * who cannot read? Again; many among

---

* Let it be kept in mind that for fifteen hundred years, that is until the art of printing was invented, hardly any of the people knew how to read. According to the Protestant theory all these people must have lived without means of obtaining faith! It is simply absurd.

them have no leisure to read, their time being wholly taken up with manual labor, and what is a book to him who has no time to read it? If Protestantism is in the right, if to attain one's salvation one needs read the Bible, then, in the words of the Lutheran Lessing, "Oh, how much do I feel for you, who are born in countries where the native language cannot render the language of the Bible! * you, who are born in these conditions of society wherefrom all knowledge is banished, and cannot therefore read the Bible! You believe yourselves Christians because you are baptized? Unhappy wretches! know, that in order to be saved, it is as much necessary for you to know how to read, as it is to have been baptized. And yet I fear you shall have to learn Hebrew that you may make your salvation perfectly sure."

And even when all the poor will have learned how to read, will they be much benefited by it? Will they not find themselves at a standstill at almost every verse of the Bible, as

---

* From scientific accounts given by learned Protestants it has been proven that it is *absolutely impossible* to translate the Bible into some languages; in which words cannot be found to render a great number of the ideas expressed in the holy Book. Then you have whole nations which can never attain faith, if it is to be attained by the reading of the Bible!

we have just said? Nor can you tell me that it will be enough for the people if their pastors will read them a lecture on the Holy Scriptures once a week! These explanations rest only on personal opinions, are not supported by any authority, and will vary according to every individual view. It is the word of God no more; it is the word of Mr. A, or of Mr. B, — quite a different affair.

Thus whether the people know how to read or not, it is absolutely impossible that the Bible should be the Rule of their Faith. Had God given the Bible for a Rule of Faith, he would have kept away from his Church and from eternal salvation almost all men; the which it is an impiety to assert, and none will ever believe it.

Then Protestantism, telling us, Take up and read the Bible; away with Church and priests; be satisfied with the word of God, as it is given in the Bible, — cannot be the religion of the people, and accordingly it cannot be, and is not the true Christianity, the religion of all.

XII. How it is impossible for a Protestant to know whether the Bible he reads be the Word of God. — I defy all Protestants, past, present, and future, to prove, without doing violence to their principles, that the Bible is truly the word of God.

As for myself, being a Catholic, the question is easily solved. I know what the Holy Scriptures are. The Church of God, the living and infallible authority established by JESUS CHRIST on earth to teach me the knowledge and practice of true faith, lays open before me the holy books, and tells me in his name: These books are the writings of the Prophets and of the Apostles. They are authentic; which means, they are indeed written by those to whom they are attributed; and are, moreover, inspired, which means, they are written with the assistance of the Holy Ghost, and they truly contain the word of God. I believe in the teaching of the Church, and, logical in my faith, I say and believe that the Bible is the word of God.

On the other hand, the Protestant, from the moment he rejects the authority of the Church, cannot reason as I do. With Bible in hand, he cannot tell you why he has faith in what it teaches.

1. Are the books of the Bible authentic? - I will ask a Protestant at once, — how do you know that they have been truly written by the Prophets and the Apostles?

Thus we are in a mesh of historical questions,

some among them almost inexplicable. Schoerer, a Protestant doctor remarks: "Each individual is here called upon to give his opinion on matters about which doctors have doubts and disagree. The most simple among the faithful must, before he can trust his faith, resolve questions of *authenticity*, *critic*, and *history*... In sooth, it is a dish of very palatable food for the mind of the faithful! Behold a rule very accessible to the mass of the Christian people!" (*La Critique et la Foi*, par E. Schoerer, of Geneva.) But no danger for us Catholics of being in such mazes. The Church avers an authenticity, the certainty whereof she transmits to her children from age to age.

2. But let us, by an impossibility, grant that a Protestant can of a surety know that all the books of the Bible have been written by the holy authors whose names they bear, will he know as well that they are actually *inspired*, and that they are not above the level of common good books?

It may, in very sooth, be, that Saint Paul, Saint John, Saint Matthew have written a number of letters, and even religious works, which were not at all inspired. Now, how can you tell, outside the infallible judgment of the

Church, which one of the writings of those authors is, or is not inspired?

Will you say that the Holy Ghost, assisting as he does every Christian, will give you the means to ascertain which books are inspired? But, then, how is that you are so little agreed with one another on this point, and Luther rejects what Calvin accepts, and Protestants to-day receive books which their fathers rejected; as for instance the Books of Daniel, Ruth, and Esther, St. James' Epistle, and that of St. Paul to the Hebrews, etc.? What more? Even on the four Gospels Protestants cannot agree, and this very day some pastors will admit only the gospel of St. Matthew, while others will receive none but that of St. John.

This question, a fundamental one if ever there was one, on the *certainty* of the inspiration of the holy books, must needs be a stumbling block to the Protestant from the moment he becomes earnest in his reasoning. In fact, it is a mortal difficulty for Protestantism.

Thus, many Protestants, wishing to reason on their faith, find that their religious edifice is based on a very dubious foundation, and thereby lose whatever remnant of belief they possessed, and fall into rationalism or indifference.

3. Let us make a third and last remark. — Suppose, then, a Protestant has obtained a certainty of the authenticity and inspiration of the Bible; how will he know that the version which he uses and distributes among his friends is *perfectly* reliable, and does not substitute, as if often happens, the erroneous interpretation of the translator for the true and not understood sense of the original?

Very few indeed know Hebrew well enough to make a good translation from it; and on the other hand we are not sure in what language some of our holy books have been originally written.

With us the authority of the Church supplies the deficiency of these impossible researches; whereas the poor Protestants, halting before these difficulties, which they cannot overcome, either give up everything, Bible, Faith, and Religion, — or their studies, pursued without direction, entangle them in the meshes of innumerable doubts, from which they escape only by falling into a negation of all truths; or, lastly, they preserve, without the aid of any reasoning, their faith in the Scriptures, do not trouble themselves with any examination of them, and on the guaranty of *Catholic tradition*, they believe in the divine inspiration of the Bible.

which Protestantism is unable to demonstrate to them. In this they are Catholics without knowing it, and happily there are many such.

Whenever a Protestant appeals to the authority of the Bible, he unwittingly invokes the authority of the Catholic Church, whose infallible testimony is indispensable in the demonstration of the divine inspiration of the Scriptures. As early as the fourth century St. Augustine protested that "he would not believe the Gospels, were he not forced to it by the authority of the Catholic Church."

XIII. How far One may be led by the Protestant Principle, that "the Bible is the Rule of Faith." — Were the Bible, interpreted according to one's pretended inspiration, the Rule of Faith, then every reader is bound in conscience to believe and do whatever he finds in his Bible.

Now, on the supposition of this principle, which is undeniably the grand principle of Protestantism, Protestants must needs approve all the abominations and impure follies of all those sects, so-called evangelical, who, from the *Anabaptists* to the *Mormons*, have dared to sanction their infamy with misunderstood texts of the Scripture. Aye, more; they are bound to acknowledge as legitimate brothers, in sooth, as true and logical Protestants, all those Mormons and Anabaptists and vile Sectarians who are the shame of humanity.

What impurities have not been committed under the sanction of those words of the Lord "increase and multiply"! A host of sectarians, following in the wake of the Anabaptists of Munster, have on the authority of those words, dared to legitimate polygamy. On some such misapplication of a text from the Gospel, Luther, Bucerus, and Melancthon have permitted Philip, the Landgrave of Hesse, to have two wives.

In the name of the Bible, of the WORD OF GOD, Luther at first incited the German peasantry to revolt against their rulers, and then, frightened at his own work, he persuaded the princes to massacre the peasants. John of Leyden found in his studies of the Bible that he should marry eleven women at once. Hermann felt himself clearly designated in the Bible as the Envoy of the Lord. Nicholas learned from it that there was no necessity of anything connected with faith, and that we must live in sin in order that grace may abound. Sympson pretends to find in the Scriptures an ordination that men should walk in the streets stark naked, to teach the rich a lesson that they must divest themselves of everything. Richard Hill justified, with the Bible in hand, adultery and manslaughter as deeds never failing to work out some good purpose, especially when joined to incest, in which case more saints are added to the earth and more blessed to the heavens!

Even on the avowal of honest Protestants, no crime or abomination has ever failed to find its pretended justification in some scriptural text interpreted outside the authority of the Church.

What must we think of a principle leading to such consequences?

XIV. IS IT TRUE THAT THE CATHOLIC CHURCH FORBIDS READING THE BIBLE?

The Church has received the deposit of the holy Scriptures from God, and nothing has she more at heart than to see her children nourished with the Divine Word, and meditating its oracles. Yet she surrounds this excellent reading with certain precautions which her maternal prudence has learned from faith and experience.

She well knows how Satan employed the holy Scriptures to tempt the Christ in the desert, and how the Scribes and Pharisees always opposed

Jesus in the name of God's word. She holds sacred and inviolable the teachings of her first Supreme Pontiff, the Prince of the Apostles, who, in reference to the holy Scriptures, warns the faithful that in "the Epistles of St. Paul are some things hard to be understood, which the unlearned and unstable wrest, as also the other Scriptures, to their own destruction." (2 Pet. iii. 16.) Hence it is by Holy Writ that the Church is directed to give her children this divine food with great prudence. But then experience also comes to the aid of faith, in a matter of so much importance, and, thus, the example of all heretics, and, above all, of modern heretics, shows most conclusively that this reading of the Bible may in some circumstances, and especially in vernacular translations, become a source of danger. Consequently, she has laid down some very simple and wise rules, not for the purpose of preventing this salutary reading, but to avert danger.

The first rule is, that we should receive both the text and the interpretation of the Scriptures from the legitimate pastors of the Church, and from them alone, "lest," as St. Peter adds, "being led away by the errors of the unwise, ye fall from your own steadfastness." (Loc. cit.)

Then the Church commands that only those

translations shall be employed which have been carefully examined and approved by the ecclesiastical authorities. Thereby the faithful are taught that what they read is indeed the word of GOD, and not the human rendering of some ignorant or dishonest translator. She wishes, moreover, that this same authority be consulted as regards the proper dispositions of mind and heart which one must possess in order to derive profit from this holy reading.

The simple announcement of these practical rules will explain their profound wisdom. They are not only wise, but they are necessary.

The Church thereby shows a far more tender regard for the holy word of GOD than those rash innovators who, under pretence of placing it within reach of every one, have trailed it in the mud, and profaned it shamefully. Only the Catholic Church respects the Bible, because she alone comprehends its sanctity and proper usage.

And let us here add, what may be new to many, namely: the holy Scriptures are far more extensively read among Catholics than they are by Protestants. At mass, *every day*, selections from the Old Testament and from the Epistles are read together with prominent portions taken from the Holy Gospels.

Many Catholics carry about their persons the New Testament or at least the Four Gospels; which practice has become a rule with seminaries. Few indeed are to be found among the clergy who do not make the reading and meditation of the Scriptures a part of their daily studies. I cannot say how much the reverend pastors of Protestant Churches read the Bible; but I know their flocks do not read it much. In many a Protestant family, parents forbid the reading thereof, certainly with good reason, as there are many passages which it would not be prudent to allow a young man or woman to read. The Bible is preëminently the Book of the Priesthood. Besides the Eucharist, it is the most precious deposit entrusted to the hands of the priests who have been charged with the salvation of souls. By its proper use they enrich the souls of the people as well as their own souls. Theirs is the mission to make it beloved and respected by everybody, to impart it to all in portions as may be required, and thus preserve to the world of God its essential character — that of Light and Life.

The respect and love which holy priests and true Catholics have for the Bible is unsurpassable. St. Charles Borromeo, Archbishop of Milan, and the great reformer of the Italian clergy in the sixteenth century, always read the Bible on his knees, and with uncovered head: once four long hours was he absorbed in this occupation. St. Philip Neri bathed with his tears the pages he knew by heart; and so also did St. Francis de Sales and St. Vincent de Paul. M. Olier, the reformer of the clergy in France, had a wonderful veneration for the book. He had it bound in covers of massive silver, and kept it in a special place, aloof from any other book; he never opened it but with his surplice on, and always on his knees, in spite of his acute infirmities. In these sentiments are French seminarians, for the most under Sulpitian charge, trained for the sanctuary.

JESUS is the manna hidden in the Scriptures. Happy are those who search for it and find it! Happy the faithful soul who, by the light of the Holy Church and of true faith, and in a spirit of piety, love, and sanctification, searches the adorable Word of GOD, and from it, as well as from the sacrament of the altar, obtains substantial food of true and solid piety!

XV. WHY DOES THE CHURCH CONDEMN BIBLE SOCIETIES? — A very pious Catholic, who, in the meditation of the Scriptures found the strongest food to support him in his religious life, asked me once "whether the Bible societies did not after all do some good, by spreading the Book by the million: why? they came to the aid of the Catholic Church! How could then Pope Gregory XVI. condemn them, and call them a *plague?*"

Doctor Leo, a German Protestant of elevated mind, says: "The Pope has qualified the Bible Societies *a plague.* Were I an Italian and a Pope I would do the same. Let us, for once, be fair enough to examine the doings of these emissaries of Anglican Societies in Catholic countries. Acting as they do without common decency, and with a shamelessness beyond endurance, — every means is available for the purpose of spreading the Bible; — they thrust it into the hands of all, even of those who are the least apt to value the gift; they spread doctrines, which only beget confusion in the minds of the people; wound morality, shake social authority and ecclesiastic order, and will only engender revolutionary movements. Biblical Societies have, in our time, been a powerful engine in the hands of those who have set Italy topsy-turvy. The Protestant zeal of England paves the road to English politics and success, Bible in hand. Verily, the Bible is the sheep's skin under which the wolf hides himself."

There you have the question solved by a Protestant. The Protestant Bible is only a false skin, in which infidelity and revolution wrap themselves.

XVI. "THE BIBLE, THE WHOLE BIBLE, NOTHING BUT THE BIBLE." — Such is the incessant cry of Protestants, small and big, against Catholics. The Bible is the whole religion! Read the Bible and you are sure to find faith and salvation! The Bible will rid you of all *Romish* superstitions! Do you pant after a religion easy, free of all superfluous baggage? Have a Bible! Do you aspire to be one of GOD's elect? Accept of this Bible, my dear sir!

False and impossible as the principle is, which makes a book, interpreted in many and opposite ways, the Rule of Faith, one may be tempted to think that Protestants accept it with reverence and reflect on its behests. Nothing of the kind; and we have only to open the Bible to see at once the glaring contrast between the Sacred Text and Protestant doctrines on some of the most important questions.

PROTESTANT BELIEF AND PROTESTANT PRACTICE.

SACRED TEXT.

The ministers say: "The Bible is the only authority in religion. Whatever man teaches, unless it is the text of the Bible, is an usurpation and a falsehood."

Jesus Christ says to his Apostles: "As the Father hath sent me, I also send you." (John xx. 21.) "All power is given to me in heaven and on earth. Going, therefore, teach ye all nations, ... teaching them to observe all things whatsoever I have commanded you." (Matthew, xxviii. 18.) "He that heareth you, heareth me; and he that despiseth you, despiseth me." (Luke x. 16.)

The ministers say: "In fact of religion, we must believe *no person* but the Bible, the pure word of God."

And St. Paul says: "Obey your prelates and be subject to them, for they watch as beings to render an account of your souls." (Heb. xiii. 17.)

The ministers say: "Bishops claim too much; their ministry is an usurped one."

And St. Paul says to the Bishops: "The Holy Ghost has placed you Bishops to rule the Church of God." (Acts xx. 28.)

The ministers say: "The Bible's meaning can be easily caught, and the very reading of it shelters us from all errors."

But St. Peter thus speaketh of St. Paul's Letters: "In all *his* Epistles are certain things hard to be understood, which the unlearned and the unstable wrest, as they do also the other Scriptures, to their own destruction." (2 Peter iii. 16.)

We know that the Saviour wrote nothing. He never told his Apostles to write; he left not a word enjoining upon the Christians to read what the Apostles might write. Hence we see that in the primitive Church they prayed, they fasted, were baptized, received holy communion, followed all the practices of religion most faithfully, and secured the salvation of their souls without reading the Gospel, which had not as yet been written. This very little remark, which we have already previously made, and *upon which we lay a particular stress*, blights, to a very considerable extent, the grand Protestant dogma that we must needs read the Scriptures in order to know religion and be saved. Well, then, what has JESUS CHRIST done to establish and to preserve religion? He has commanded his Apostles to preach: that's all. The Apostles thought fit to put in writing some of the teaching they had received, and some of the most striking facts in the life of their Divine Master, — that is the whole of the Gospels. The balance of those teachings and of those · facts they have only delivered by word of mouth. They wrote them not on paper: they are the TRADITION. Hence TRADITION has in itself as much authority as the GOSPEL. Let us now take up the text, and examine whether the saying of ministers is in accordance with the saying of the Scriptures: —

The ministers say: "We'll have none of traditions."	St. Paul says: "Brethren, ... hold the Traditions, which you have learned, whether by word, or by our Epistle." (2 Thess. ii. 14.)
The ministers say: "All that Jesus has done or said is found in the Gospel."	St. John says at the close of his Gospel: "There are also many other things which JESUS did, which, if they were written

The ministers say: "There is no more of the Apostles' doctrine than what they have written."	every one, the world itself, I think, would not be able to contain the books that should be written." (xxi. 25.) St. Paul says to the Bishop Timothy: "The things which thou hast heard of me by many witnesses, the same commend to faithful men, who shall be fit to teach others also." (2 Tim. ii. 2.) And St. John: "I had many things to write unto thee; but I could not by ink and pen write to thee. But I hope speedily to see thee, and we will speak mouth to mouth." (2. i. 14.)
The ministers say: "Justification and salvation are to be obtained only by faith. Works are useless and without any efficacy."	St. James says: "What shall it profit, my brethren, if a man say he hath faith, but hath not works? Shall faith be able to save him?.... So faith also, if it have not works, is dead in itself.... Was not Abraham, our father, justified by works, offering up his son upon the altar?.... Do you see that by works a man is justified; and not by faith only?" (2. ii. 14, and seq.).

In the days of the Reformation, an engraver represented the institution of the Eucharist. [*A copy of it can be seen in the Library of Georgetown College.*] There is our Divine Lord distributing the Holy Sacrament to the Apostles, and by his sacred lips are uttered these words: "*This* IS *my body.*" On the right Luther offers the holy communion, and says: "*In this* IS CONTAINED *my body.*" At the left, Calvin does the same, and declares: "*This* IS THE FIGURE *of my body.*" At the bottom of the picture the engraver wrote in prominent letters, WHOM SHALL WE BELIEVE? There is a great truth, expressed with impressive eloquence, in those words.

The ministers say: "The Saviour never meant to give his own flesh for our food. It is an error forged by the Romish church."	Our Lord said: "I am the bread of life... the bread that cometh down from heaven: that if any man eateth of it, he may not die... If any man eat of this bread, he shall live forever; and the bread that I will give is my flesh, for the life of the world. The Jews therefore strove among themselves, saying: How can this man give himself to eat? Then Jesus said to them: Amen, amen, I say unto you; except you eat the flesh of the Son of man, and drink his blood, you shall not have life in you... for my flesh is meat indeed, and my blood is drink indeed." (John vi. 35, et seq.)
The ministers say: "God alone forgives sins. He has given no power to men to forgive them.'	JESUS CHRIST says to his messengers: "Receive ye the Holy Ghost. Whose sins you shall forgive, they are forgiven them; and whose sins you shall retain, they are retained." — (John xx. 22.) And: "Amen, I say to you, whatsoever you shall bind upon earth, shall be bound also in heaven." (Matt. xviii. 18.)

Nothing easier than to continue this parallel. It sets forth the great opposition between the teaching of the ministers and that *Word of God* which said ministers vaunt so much to follow as the only Rule of Faith. In the face of such incontrovertible truths, what becomes of the great Protestant principle, — the Bible, the whole Bible?

No wonder that Protestants, startled by such incongruities, end by rejecting the Bible altogether, inasmuch as they cannot base their belief on it any more. Many parsons look upon the Bible as man's work. "We cannot deny," says M. Coquerel, "that the holy books contain contradictions, and errors in point of fact." (*Lien*, May 6th, 1852.) The Mayor of Berlin, addressing the king in behalf of the Protestantism of the city, said: "As for the majority of Protestants, the Bible and the symbolic books only bear witness to the labors in establishing Christianity; they are *works purely human;* they contain not what may be called an absolute truth." (*Memoire sur l'Instruction publique en Allemagne*, par E. RENDU.) To finish this picture, Professor Schoerer of Geneva, calls the holy Scriptures, A VENTRILOQUISM CABALISTIC. (*La Critique et la Foi*, pp. 20, 22.)

There! you have what Protestants have made of the Bible.

XVII. THE CATHOLIC PRIEST, AND THE PROTESTANT MINISTERS.— People, especially in Europe, have a very erroneous idea of Protestant ministers. They look upon them as a sort of priests, endowed with a special and sacred character, which distinguishes them from all other persons and gives them authority in matters of religion. Hence many offset Protestantism and its parsons against the Church and her priests. It is a preposterous idea; yet it is worth its while to dwell a little upon it.

What is a priest? He is a man consecrated exclusively to God, by the sacrament of order, which he receives by the imposition of the hands of the Bishop, and gives him, in the name of our Lord JESUS CHRIST, a character holy and indelible, the power and charge of teaching religion to men, celebrating the holy Sacrifice, pardoning sins, and sanctifying the faithful. By the sacrament of order, the priest receives a participation of the very power of *Jesus Christ* over souls. He is made priest forever, and will remain priest forever, even in spite of himself; so much so that his power and the sanctity of his ministry are absolutely independent of his personal qualities.

Let us turn the other way, and see what a Protestant minister is. A difficult question, this; for, like Protestantism, the Protestant minister is a veritable Proteus, slipping from your grasp when you feel sure of having a good hold of him. It is not the same minister in

Paris as it is in New York. The definition that fits him in London will not suit the latitude of Berlin.

Yet, amidst this prodigious variety of the *species*, the *genus* remains, and in its general outlines it has been thus defined by Count de Maistre: "A Protestant minister is a gentleman dressed in black, who, on a Sunday, delivers from a pulpit some fine talk."

For my part, I would say with more severity, that "A heretical minister is a man who takes upon himself the sinful charge of attacking, in the name of the Gospel, the Church of Jesus Christ, and of spreading or maintaining error in the midst of men."

I say "they take upon themselves," because God has not commissioned them. God has sent to men the pastors of his Church, and he has promised to be with them, *even to the consummation of the world.* Such is the divine mission, the only true pastoral and evangelical mission. The hand of fellowship, nominations by consistories, salaries by government, cannot confer a religious character, cannot give a divine mission. Nothing can take the place of the Holy Ghost, or of the sacrament of Order.

I say, moreover, that the heretical minister is culpable, indeed; very much so. For he attacks the work of Jesus Christ, he attacks the true faith, and falls under the anathema pronounced by St. Paul against all men who preach doctrines at variance with those of the Church. Nill-he-will-he, be he in good faith or bad faith, the Protestant minister does a very bad work, robbing the Christian of that *faith*, which is the foundation of salvation.

Protestant pastors may have virtues, but that does not alter the question. It is their ministry which is perverse, not their persons. To what rare qualities and talents they may possess, we will grant our personal esteem, by all means. Yet their anti-Catholic work is none the less detestably impious, and worthy the condemnation of every Christian soul. Superficial minds get generally puzzled by these two things: the form makes them forget the substance; and in the man they ignore the heretic.

Will you know what, in fact, gives power to Protestant ministers? It is not their words, nor their doctrines, nor their virtues, but the *Catholic instinct, deeply true, and surviving in the heart of Protestants, unknown to themselves, for an authority visible, living, and teaching in matters of religion.* In this, as in everything else, Protestantism subsists only in what it has received from Catholicity. It is heart-rending, however, to see poor souls, often true and honest, at the mercy of men without fixed religious principles, tossed by every wind, and very often without even a belief in our Lord JESUS CHRIST.

It would be an insult to the Catholic clergy to compare with them the pastors of Protestant sects. As Protestantism is no religion, whatever they may say to the contrary, so its ministers have not the authority of the *priesthood*, no matter how hard they may try to have its appearance.

[I deem it useless to institute here a comparison between our missionaries and those who are called Protestant missionaries. It is well known (especially since Mr. Marshall's work on the *Missions* has been published) how null and futile those pretended missions have been, and how its agents have been more interested in cotton and opium than in promoting the glory of God. Besides their own welfare, those agents of Foreign Missions work only to put every obstacle in the way of success for our martyr-apostles.]

XVIII. HOW THE PRIEST IS THE MEDIATOR BETWEEN GOD AND MEN.—Often have Protestant ministers, in the footsteps of Rousseau and Voltaire, taunted the Catholic priests for stepping between God and man, and intercepting the communications between the Creator and the creature. The reproach would have some foundation had the priest assumed so much without a mission, as, in fact, ministers do. The priest does not usurp, but he fulfils a duty and asserts a right, in obedience to Him who has sent them forth to preach the true religion, to fight error, to sanctify and save souls, to reconcile the sinner, to dispense among the faithful the mysteries of God.

Again: the priests, the ministers of the Church, do not intercept communications between JESUS CHRIST and the Christian souls, no more than He intercepted, in his lifetime, communications between the Divinity and the world. On the contrary, God spoke to men through the Humanity of Christ, and taught them and blessed them; and that humanity was the means divinely instituted to establish religion. That is the bond that unites man to God.

Now, the mystery of the Church on earth being the continuation and extension of the mystery of the incarnation, it is no wonder if JESUS CHRIST, having ascended to heaven, and being invisible in his glory, still employs "humanity" to finish his work.

He exerts his power through his apostles; he is everything in his priests, who are nothing without him. Through the Pope he governs and infallibly teaches his Church; through the bishops and priests he is the pastor of souls; and when Protestants charge the Church with an usurpation of God's rights, they only exhibit a total ignorance of the mystery of salvation.

XIX. LEARNING AND CONTROVERSY OF PROTESTANT MINISTERS. — At first sight, Protestant ministers appear to be very learned men; but by following them close, very little solidity is to be found in their learning, which is all Protestant, — that is, *negative;* it is a belligerent knowledge, not inspired by the hallowing love of truth, but by the powerful hatred of whatever is Catholic.

In dispute and controversy, they bring along an interminable array of books, quotations, texts, facts, and dates. The audience, dazzled by such light (?), feel disposed to think that the gentlemen are really prodigies of learning.

Nothing of the kind. There are exceptions, indeed, and I know some distinguished men among them, hard students. You will find them in Germany, and among the *High Church* men of England; and some in this country. Their studies lead them nearer and nearer to Catholic faith. Willing as we earnestly are to render homage to men learned and friendly to truth, we must say that they are few in number. In France, the erudition of ministers is confined, generally speaking, to a certain number of passages from the writings of the Fathers, garbled after the *minister's own view;* some facts of doubtful authenticity, apparently in opposition with some Catholic dogma, or practice; lastly, a thundering storm of quotations from the Bible.

We cannot be fooled by such people. Hundreds and thousands of times have those objections, the same which Martin Luther offered, been refuted, in a most conclusive way, by Bellarmin, and Suarez, and St. Francis de Sales, and Fenelon, and Bossuet, etc., etc., etc. For the lack of better weapons, they tread on the same ground over and over.

It must be admitted that unless one's studies have been extensive, and unless one is endowed with an extraordinary memory, a well-instructed Catholic, and even a priest, can be very easily startled by a *telling* quotation. The least chance for examination or research would very easily afford a reply; but the discussion allows of no respite, and the momentary embarrassment is proclaimed a defeat. There is honesty for you.

From what we have said it can be very easily understood why the Church, sure as she is of possessing divine truth in her doctrine, and of the futility of heretical assertions, commands her children to keep clear of controversies with Protestant ministers, and forbids us to listen to their sermons or to read their books, without a special authorization. It is no fear on her part; it is prudence, and prudence begets security.

XX. WHY DO NOT CATHOLIC PRIESTS MARRY AS PROTESTANT MINISTERS DO? — Once a Protestant minister reproached a young student for his misconduct; to which the latter replied: "Very easy for you to talk so, sir. Luther has declared that it is as impossible to keep from marriage, as to go about without clothes, or live without nourishment; after this, his opinion, you have married. I would marry too, had I the means; but I am only twenty, and the government and the *evangelical societies* give me nothing, as yet, wherewith to keep house; so, meanwhile, I do the best I can."

It would prove interesting to know what reply was given by a parson married on the Protestant principle, that celibacy is against nature.

A Catholic priest would have replied: "*Be ye followers of me, as I also am of Christ*" (1 Cor. xi. 1). Be chaste, as I am, and say not that it is impossible, because, what one can do another also can.

Celibacy enables the priest to devote himself wholly to his ministry. On embracing the ecclesiastical state priests pledge themselves with free will, and, after due probation, to observe perfect continence. Although this obligation is not a divine institution, it is, nevertheless, one of marvellous wisdom. The Church well knew what she was about, when she changed the *evangelic* and apostolic *counsel* of celibacy into an absolute command for her priests;* and the devil knows very well what he is about when he protests against this salutary institution.

Were our priests married, do you think they would sacrifice themselves as they do every

---

* It is but proper to observe here, that if married men were ordained Catholic priests, in the first ages of the Church, no ordained priest was allowed to marry after he had been elevated to the dignity of the priesthood.

day? Do you not believe they would hesitate before they entered a place of loathing and contagion, and leave directions concerning their bank accounts with next kin and neighbor? And who are the kin and kith of a married man but his wife and children?

It is out of the question. We can never be reconciled with the idea of a Catholic priest being married. Christian priesthood and the wife's teakettle will never harmonize. The Protestant parsonship, which after all is only a caricature of the priesthood, drags after itself its household like a cumbrous cannon-ball. Nothing more laughable than what a certain pastor, Mr. Bost, tells of himself in his *Memoirs*.* The history of his apostolic excursions, of his preaching, of his divers *vocations*, of his change of *convictions*, is interlarded with ludicrous histories of matrimonial cares, of tin pans, and cooking-stoves. With his wife, eleven children, two servants, one piano, and two canary-birds, the unfortunate apostle parades all around, for fifteen or twenty years, *thirteen thousand pounds* of evangelic baggage.

---

* *Mémoires pouvant servir à l'histoire du réveil religieux des Eglises Protestantes de la Suisse et de la France, et à l'intelligence des principales questions theologiques et ecclesiastiques de nos jours, etc., etc.* Par A. Bost, Ministre Protestant.

How vividly all this represents primitive Christianity, Saint Paul and his staff!

XXI. HOW OUR SAVIOUR AND HIS APOSTLES DIFFER ON THE POINT OF SACERDOTAL CELIBACY FROM PROTESTANT MINISTERS. — Few questions are better defined *by the Bible* than that of religious celibacy. The church only repeats what our Saviour and his great apostle, Saint Paul, have taught on this delicate subject.

The Pharisees question JESUS about marriage, and our Lord solemnly proclaims its indissolubility. The apostles, alarmed at the hard condition of married folks, consult him in their turn: "If the case of a man with his wife be so, it is not expedient to marry." "But," he said to them, "not all take this word, but they to whom it is given." Then he adds: "There are such who deprive themselves of marriage *for the kingdom of heaven. He who can take* it, let him take it." (Matt. xix. 10, etc.)

It seems as if the ministers, although very evangelical, are not of those *to whom it is given* to *take the word;* whereof our priests, papists though they be, ignorant as they are said to be of the genuine word of GOD, *take it.* They understand the counsel of the Master, and have heart enough to follow it.

The doctrine of virginity and celibacy is none the less beautifully defined by St. Paul, in his first epistle to the Corinthians, seventh chapter. The principles are so distinctly set down that Mme. de Gasparin, in her anti-Catholic zeal, declares, with charming ingenuity, that it is *evident* that such passages of the epistle as refer to celibacy are not inspired. "Inspiration returns," says she, "when St. Paul passes to other subjects."

Well, the apostle says: "*Now concerning virgins I have no commandment of the Lord; but I give counsel, as having obtained mercy of the Lord, to be faithful.*" Just what the Catholic Church teaches; she forces no person to a life of celibacy. True, she makes a law of this counsel, a strict law for her ministers, but she forces no one to embrace the priesthood; and when a Christian expresses his intention to become priest, he acts on his perfectly free will, and it is only on his spontaneous determination that he accepts the condition of a perfect chastity.

The motives of this conduct of the Church will be also found in St. Paul. After showing that matrimony is good and honorable, he adds: "*I would have you without solicitude. He who is unmarried, careth for the things of the Lord, how he may please God. But he who is married is solicitous about the things of the world, how he may please his wife, and he is divided. And the unmarried woman and the virgin thinketh of the things of the Lord, that she may be holy in body and spirit. But she that is married, thinketh of the things of the world, how she may please her husband."* And the apostle concludes thus: *" Therefore both he that giveth his virgin in marriage, doth well; and he who giveth her not,* DOTH BETTER." *Bene facit;* MELIUS FACIT.

There is the argument summed up. Marriage is good, celibacy is better. What have the ministers to say to this? It is not I that speaketh, but the Bible. Let us be candid. They care naught for the Bible, but they detest the priests, the only true ministers of the Gospel. They wish them to marry, that they may be *unpriested.* They are chagrined, because they cannot deprive them of that angelic celibacy, which crowns them with a holy halo, and justly secures to them the confidence and the veneration of the people.

Cunning Philistines, they would like to rob Samson of his strength, through their Delilahs! But, warned by the example of the first Samson, the latter will not give in. They reject Delilah, and fight against the enemies of GOD's people the unconquerable battles of faith.

XXII. ABOUT THE JESUITS. — Calvin looked upon the members of the Company of Jesus as his most deadly enemies, and said that it was necessary to get rid of them. In his usual impudent style he wrote: "They must be destroyed, and if it cannot be done quietly, they must be chased away, or crushed under the weight of falsehoods and calumnies." *Jesuitæ vero qui se maxime nobis opponunt, aut necandi, aut, si hoc commode fieri non potest, ejiciendi, aut certe mendaciis et calumniis opprimendi sunt.*

The children of Calvin, and, in later times, the followers of Voltaire, have most piously and most faithfully taken up the cry, and have been so industrious, and have lied so skilfully, have so terribly slandered the Jesuits, that they have succeeded in making a number of people believe that those holy priests are only impostors, hypocrites, villains, conspirators, traitors, obscurantists, assassins, perverse and dangerous men.

Is it necessary to assert that the Jesuits are nothing of the kind? They are grave and admirable religious people, burning with zeal, indefatigable in the service of the Church and of souls, always ready to help a good work. They are in the Church a chosen troop. Protestants and infidels know it well. Hence they detest them, and have been heaping on them every kind of calumny for the last three hundred years, with a will, and with all their power.

I have at command a mass of eulogies bestowed on the Jesuits by Protestants whose partiality in their favor cannot be suspected. But I will only quote the spirited as well as most conclusive testimony of Henry IV. To the Parliament and to the University of Paris, who had charged the Jesuit Fathers with all the crimes, for which they have been constantly and perseveringly traduced ever since, he replied:—

"I thank you for the care which you take in behalf of my person and of my State. You say, the Sorbonne has condemned the Jesuits; but it was done, as in your case, before it had known them; and if the old Sorbonne did not act from jealousy, the new one has improved on the old, and boasts of it.

"You say that the most learned among the members of your Parliament have learned nothing of them; if the most learned are the oldest among you, it is true, for they have made their studies before the Jesuits were known in France. If the best studies are made among you, how does it happen, that, in consequence of their absence, your university is become deserted, and that students flock, in spite of your orders, to Douay, to Pont-à-Mousson, and to places out of the kingdom?

"Again you say, that they draw the youth of fine disposition and make choice of the best: for this I think the more of them. Do we not choose the best of soldiers to fight our battles?

"You say, they come in the best way they can. So does everybody; and have I not entered my kingdom the best way I could? At the same time we must acknowledge that they are possessed of an admirable patience, and I, for one, admire it, for with patience and good life they achieve everything.

"You say, that they are great sticklers for their institute; that is just what will preserve them. Thus I would change none of their rules, and thus I wish them to keep them.

"As for the ecclesiastics, who find fault with them, it is the old story of ignorance assailing learning, and I know very well that when I spoke of re-establishing them, two kinds of people particularly opposed me; those who belong to the so-called reformed religion and ecclesiastics of dubious morals. Just what made me think more of them."

The Jesuits have always been persecuted and will always be. Their founder has besought for them, on his death-bed, the crown promised by the Lord in his sermon of the mountain, touching the eighth beatitude, — "Blessed are those who suffer persecution for justice' sake; for theirs is the kingdom of heaven. Blessed are ye, when men shall revile you, and persecute you, and speak all that is evil against you, untruly for my sake. Be glad and rejoice, for your reward is great in heaven." — (Matt. v. 10, etc.)

There you have the history of the Company of Jesus written in advance of its existence. The special hatred with which heretics and infidels have always persecuted its members is their best eulogy.

XXIII. MIXED MARRIAGES. — When one party is Catholic and the other is not, the marriage is called *mixed*.

The Church grieves at such marriages. They exhibit great indifference in matter of religion, and often entail the non-Catholic training of the offspring. For my part, I cannot understand how a Christian, a Catholic, can be so forgetful of objects divine, as to choose for a companion in life a heretical woman, to be the mother of his children, the directress of his domestic life.

The Church leaves no means untried to make us feel how repugnant these marriages are to her. She refuses them the enhancing majesty of her wedding ritual, and positively forbids her ministers to take any other part in them but that of a *witness*. Hence such marriages are contracted outside the Church, in the vestry, — no blessing, no prayer, no holy water, no surplice, no stole. Moreover, the betrothed, on both sides, must bind themselves, beforehand, and under a solemn oath, to raise in the Catholic Church *all* the children that may issue from their marriage, both boys and girls. Unless this oath is taken, the Church will not permit a mixed marriage to be contracted.

When you then meet the child of a mixed marriage raised in Protestantism, know that the parents have perjured themselves.

And were even all conditions requisite for such deplorable unions fulfilled, and the matrimonial bond signed before a priest, let it be known that the Catholic party is forbidden to go before a Protestant parson. It would be a participation with heretics *in sacred* things, and a culpable allowance in favor of heresy.* Once married in the Catholic Church, what do you need at the meeting-house? Not the matrimonial bond, for you are already joined in it. If you only go for the purpose of hearing some fine passages of the Bible relating to matrimony, it is not worth the scandal you give, and you can as well read them at home.

Protestants, you know, do not consider matrimony a sacrament, and if the reverend gentlemen still insist upon "couples" coming before them, it is for the sake of a fee.

Mixed marriages are a token of weakened faith. No Christian will ever stoop to such a religious incongruity, unless he be lost to all sentiments of Catholic dignity.

Matrimony is a great sacrament; on it generally depends the happiness and salvation of husband and wife. Woe to them who do not contract it according to God's laws, and let family arrangements, wealth, and sentimentality trample on their faith!

---

* The Catholic party must also promise to do everything, by word and example, to bring about the conversion of the non-Catholic. — Tr.

PART THIRD.

1. WHAT PREVENTS HONEST PROTESTANTS FROM BECOMING CATHOLICS? — The ignorance of the teachings of the Church, an almost unconquerable prejudice against the Church, the stronger because imbibed at their mothers' breast, confirmed by education, and never combated. With the best faith in the world, they look upon the Church as a school of superannuated superstitions;* her holy authority a tyranny, an usurpation; her priests cunning fellows who cheat the people; her children so many dolts who believe whatever they are told to believe.

Bossuet, after having battled with the ablest

---

* "Lifeless ceremonial and senseless mummery; superstitions of the Romish Church; dictatorship of the hierarchy; unscriptural creeds; gross doctrines; irrational mysteries, etc.," are some of the qualifications attributed to the Catholic Church by Mr. J. T. Bixby, "CHRISTIAN EXAMINER," Boston, July, 1867, pp. 77, 78.

ministers of his time, came to the conclusion that ignorance was the greatest obstacle in the way of conversion from Protestantism. After such an experience he published his *Exposition of the Catholic Doctrine*, which took all ministers by surprise. Astonished to find dogmas, qualified, by them, as ridiculous and superstitious, so simple, so evident, so great, they charged Bossuet with having disguised the truth to serve his cause. Whereupon he submitted his work to the Pope, and to almost all the Bishops of France, and published a second edition with an authentic approbation of the Holy See, and of about fifty Bishops. It brought back to the Church the great Turenne, the Marquis de Dangeau, grandson of that Duplessis-Mornay who was called the *Pope of Huguenots*, together with a train of distinguished men.

The ignorance of Protestants in regard to Catholic doctrine is beyond all belief. Do they not assert that we *worship* the Blessed Virgin, look upon her as a goddess, attribute to her a divine power? Do not many among them charge us with *adoring* the Pope, selling the Body and Blood of Christ, setting a tariff on confession, and affirm such absurdities as they should be ashamed to impute to men of sense and education?

The *Catechism* is the most available book to place in the hands of Protestants, — the book we put in the hands of children.

2. About the idolatrous Adorations, with which Protestants reproach Catholics. — "Catholics allow creatures the adorations they owe to the Creator," — an oft-repeated charge made in pamphlets and books by the parsons, and re-echoed from their pulpits. We may repeat it over and again, that the Catholics adore only God; no use, — they *know* we are idolators, duly convicted, no more nor less than the Hottentots and the Cochin-Chinese.

Yet let us protest once more: We adore God, God alone, — we adore our Lord Jesus Christ, because he is God, — we adore neither the Virgin Mary nor the saints, — we honor and venerate them, we give them what is due to the mother and friends of our Lord and King. We beseech them to pray for us, because their prayers are more worthy and more acceptable to God than ours. What can be more simple? It must needs be an evil-minded spirit that will find in it an occasion for launching anathema against the Church.

The malignant slander that we *adore* the Pope is too ridiculous to deserve an answer.

They force themselves into seeing an adoration in every genuflection of ours. They exhibit no great proof of good sense in that. We go on our knees, because the humble and devout posture of the body has an influence over the soul, and disposes it to a prayer more recollected, and to a religion more profound. Who ignores the great influence of the body over the soul?

It is, moreover, very natural, that a heart penetrated with reverence, humility, and repentance, should bring the body to bend low, and thus agree in the worship of the spirit.

It is thus that we love to kneel, not only before our Lord JESUS CHRIST, to adore and beseech him, but even at the feet of his Blessed Mother, whom we respect so much, before the honored relics of martyrs and saints, and before the sacred image of the cross. In his law GOD does not forbid to *venerate* holy things; but he forbids to *worship* them. No Catholic will ever be found who adores a picture of Mary, a crucifix, or a relic, thereby confounding GOD with them?*

---

* Protestants forever din our ears quoting Moses: "*Thou shalt not make to thyself a graven thing*,"—but scarcely

Let us then go on our knees, with an humble love, before the hallowed objects of the true worship of the true GOD; and likewise at the feet of the Vicar of our Lord JESUS CHRIST, at the feet of Bishops and of God's priests, that we may receive their holy blessing; which is not the benediction of man, but of JESUS who dwells in them, and who, through them, blesses, enlightens, and sanctifies the world.

III. A WORD ABOUT PROTESTANT PAMPHLETS AND TRACTS.—With two kinds of tracts do Biblical Societies overflow the land.

First, and the more numerous, contain insipid tales, of a clammy and languid religiosity, wherein we are invariably treated with conversions performed at the mere sight of the Bible, women dying a most holy death, without confession, sacraments, or priest; an everlasting sanctimonious parson, very tolerant, with a honeyed and Biblical tongue; or a dame, very religious, all zeal for the Gospel, running from hut to hut, comforting the poor with a chapter of the Bible. In these tracts the Catholic

---

ever add the words "*to adore them.*" We adore them no more than the Israelites adored the two golden cherubs which Moses had placed, by the order of GOD himself, on either side of the Ark of the Covenant.

Church is not openly attacked. Oh, no! The danger is only negative. It lies in that the ideas of the readers are puzzled by having presented to their admiration and imitation examples of a religion altogether opposed to genuine Christianity. The very silence about the Catholic Church is an attack made in perfidiousness. This premeditated silence, vaunted as a part of moderation, is inimical; and it has a purpose, — it leads people to ignore the Church, and let it slide. Happily, these stories are badly written, and mortally sickening; for which GOD should be thanked.

Tracts belonging to the *second* class are distributed with more judgment, and boldly attack the Holy Church. They are, for the most, violent disquisitions on what religion holds most venerable and holy; shameless calumnies against the clergy, blasphemies against the Mother of GOD, and falsehoods so revolting that they cannot be attributed to mere ignorance. As we read in a solemn warning by the Bishop of Strasbourg, they bear, at times, a Catholic title, and, to cover the snare, are adorned with pictures of Our Lady.

Protestants look upon the spreading of these tracts as a meritorious work, carried on with great unanimity by divided sects. They as-same increased proportions every year. The old carrier, who formerly went about carrying his bundle, is transformed and multiplied. The fair sex becomes every day more and more interested in the enterprise. Rail-road cars are thronged with *evangelists* in petticoats. Cramming their pockets, their work-baskets, their bandboxes, with tracts written by their respective parsons, these women start for the crusade, determined to destroy the empire of superstition. They offer their little papers, distribute them, cast them abroad, intrude them upon you, or drop them. They slide them through Venetian blinds, thrust them under doors, and pin them on rails, or on trees, on the highways.

Nor is this a newfangled apostolate. Luther was not ashamed to follow it. He added the sting of caricature to the defamatory libel which he would write in the heat of his imagination, and with a system led by a genius not less malicious than brutal. Melancthon, the *angelic*, his favorite disciple, was his chief assistant in this cowardly business. Libels were they, and caricatures, prompted by such noble motives, and written in a revolting and sickening style. Although certain slippery points, upon which Luther could, so naturally, balance himself well, are somewhat roughened in modern tracts, yet we prefer to believe that those devout travellers, anxious as they are to thrust them upon the people, do not read them beforehand.

IV. HOW CERTAIN PROTESTANT PAMPHLETEERS SHOULD LEARN THE ART OF VERIFYING DATES. — Among those pamphlets which covertly attack Catholicity, some pretend to be able to silence the Catholic Church forever, by convicting it of innovation, and quote the *precise, absolutely verified* date of the *invention* of each Catholic dogma.

This practice would not be, after all, so very disastrous to them, were they only able to agree with each other; whereas, they contradict each other, and baffle each other's schemes. As they quote dates at hap-hazard, only a miracle could help them to meet on one and the same point.. Let us take up two chronologies, one published in England, by Bulington and Bulton Horncastle, with the title, *Dates of the new Doctrines added to the Church of Rome*, the other published in Angers, A. D. 1846, by the facetious Rev. Mr. Puaux, under the title, *Extracts of Origins.*

Now see how these two historians of *good faith* agree together: —

The English Historian.		*The Rev. Parson Puaux.*	
Invocation of Saints Invented in	700	Worship of Saints Invented in	875
Supremacy of the Pope,	1215	Primacy of the Pope,	600
Apocrifical Books,	1547	Apocrifical Books,	1564
Seven Sacraments,	1547	Seven Sacraments,	1160

And so on. Indeed, "*Iniquity hath lied to itself.*" (Ps. xxvi. 12.)

Outside the Puaux chronology, there are other dates established with uniformity enough to fix the origin of the pretended *additions* made to our dogmas and religious practices.

Thus, as regards confession, which has been their constant bugbear, they fix the institution thereof in the year of grace 1215, and the dogma of the Immaculate Conception in the year 1854. They throw those dates into our faces with an air of triumph, and exclaim, "That's the way your dogmas are manipulated."

There is nothing so mean, and at the same time so impudent, as half-learning. Protestants well-instructed are very chary in making such foolish assertions; for they know, as well as we, that, in 1215, Pope Innocent III., in the Lateran Council, only established certain rules in reference to the annual approach to the sacrament of penance, — a sacrament instituted by our Divine Saviour, and practised since the beginning of the Church; and they know that, in 1854, the Supreme Pontiff Pius IX. did not invent the belief that Mary was free from the stain of original sin; but he only proclaimed and made obligatory for all to believe the ancient doctrine of the Church. The dogma of the Immaculate Conception existed before the proclamation, even as it now exists. In fact, the feast thereof was celebrated in all Christendom, from time immemorial, with only this difference, that it had not been *officially defined*, and one might be deceived on the point of this doctrine without becoming heretic, as, in fact, many were deceived, who otherwise were great men, and even saints, and nourished the most ardent and the deepest love for our blessed Lady.

We might as well say that the Council of Nice invented the dogma of the Trinity, and that of the Divinity of the Word, when, in 325, it *defined* these two great truths against the Arians. Before the Nicene Council, the Church believed both the Trinity and the Incarnation, the same as she believed the sacrament of confession before the Council of Lateran, and the

Immaculate Conception of the mother of our Lord before the eighth of December, 1854.

The Catholic dogma is the truth religious. But truth is not made, it *exists* eternal and immutable. The Church is the depository thereof, and, guided by her divine chief, our Lord, she proclaims her teachings accordingly as innovators dare deny them, or whenever she thinks proper to do so for the good of her children.

V. PROTESTANT TOLERATION. — Among the many prejudices which sway the world, and reign even among demi-Catholics, one is, "although the Reformation may have been the cause of evil, may have caused man's blood to flow, and may have demoralized whole nations, it has, at least, done this much good: *it has given religious toleration.*"

Nothing farther from truth, or less sustained by history. Wherever Protestantism has a sway, it is intolerant and persecuting. Of course not everywhere, in the same degree; but why not? Because it does not possess everywhere the same degree of power. To persecute, one must have both will and power. Fortunately Protestantism cannot always act as it has a mind to. But let it be said boldly, in fact, of intolerance, Protestantism will always go as far as it will dare.

The Reformation has always introduced itself by violence, and its first fruits, in Germany, Geneva, England, and Sweden, have been civil war, proscription, and murder. How else? The Reformation is a revolution, and whatever is revolutionary, is, of its own nature, tyrannical.

Once established, Protestantism has held its own by the same dint of violence. Everybody knows in what relation English Protestantism stands to the Catholics, — how bloody the laws, and with what ferocious despotism it crushes, this very day, faithful and unhappy Ireland.

William Cobbett, a Protestant writer, in the face of such facts could not give the lie to his conscience, and he thus testifies against the national Church: "A Church," he writes, "the most intolerant that ever existed, rampant before the world, with knife, and axe, and the instruments of cruel torture; its first steps marked with the blood of numberless victims, whilst its arm gave way under the burden of its robberies." Then he quotes the acts of Parliament, by which it is proven that in consequence of this wholesale butchery of Catholics, the population of England was diminished *one-tenth* its number. *Death* was proclaimed against any priest who should dare to enter the kingdom, or who should be convicted of having celebrated mass. *Death* for him who gave shelter to a priest. *Death* to every one who refused to acknowledge Queen Elizabeth at the Head of the Church of JESUS CHRIST. A heavy fine imposed on all who refused to assist at the Protestant service, and " the list of all those who were put to death, for the only crime of being Catholics, during the reign of Elizabeth, would be by far more numerous than the roll of our armies and of our navy," adds the same historian.

"Nor is the English Church changed; it has proven true to itself from the very first beginning of its existence; its cruelties in Ireland would degrade, in atrocity, those of Mohammed himself, and a whole volume should be required to chronicle all its acts of intolerance." (Lettre to Tenderden, Lord Justice, who, in Parliament, had boasted of the tolerance of the British government.)

By the same means did Calvinism introduce itself into France. For more than one century we hear nothing in that country but rebellions, and riots, and devastation, wherever the Huguenot doctrine gained admittance. That period is only a tissue of disorders, treachery, and cruelty. Nor is there cause for wonder, when Calvin publicly proclaimed that kings and princes must be broken, when they refuse the profession of Protestantism; *better to spit in their faces than to obey them.* Under the guidance of Coligny, the Calvinistic revolutionists planned the project of abducting the King of France, yet an infant. Having failed, they took possession of Orleans, laid waste the borders of the Loire, Normandy, and the Island of France. Languedoc fared the worst of all, as it became the theatre of cruelties and profanations unparalleled in history. At Montauban, Castres, Beziers, Nîmes, and Montpellier, those vaunted pioneers of tolerance, and liberty of conscience forbade, under terrible penalties, all practice of Catholic worship. The world has heard of that notorious Baron des Adrets, a Calvinian leader, who, after the surrender of Montbrison, indulged in the innocent pleasure of hurling from the highest tower the surviving defenders of the post. Thus did generally fare all cities that fell into Calvinistic hands: churches desecrated, sacred vessels stolen, priests and monks driven away or killed, most barbarous atrocities committed and sacrileges most abominable. These are historical facts; they challenge contradiction, and are not denied even by

Protestants, who, however, from time to time allow themselves to be caught wishing the return of the good old Protestantism of France.

It makes one's hair stand on end to read the atrocities whereof the Hollanders became guilty when striving to extend Protestantism over the Netherlands; above all, the tortures and torments with which Lamark and Sonoi, agents of the Prince of Orange, gave vent to their *religious zeal*. We have a faithful picture of Sonoi drawn by a Protestant pen: "The ordinary processes of cruel torture were only the lowest degree of punishment inflicted on the innocent. Their limbs were disjointed; the flesh, hanging in shreds, after a pitiless scourging, was swathed in rags dipped in alcohol, then set on fire, until, the flesh burnt and the nerves crisped, the bones were bared to view. Sometimes so much as half a pound of sulphur was employed in burning the armpits and the soles of their feet. Thus martyred, they were abandoned on the fields for days and nights without any relief, only that repeated blows drove sleep away from their eyes. No food given but herrings, or such as would create a burning thirst, whilst no kind of drink, no, not even water, was allowed. Hornets were inserted to sting their navels. Sonoi went so far as to cause rabid rats to be placed on the breasts and bellies of those martyrs, enclosed in a box made for the purpose, and covered with combustibles. Fire being applied, these vermin became furious, and would cleave a way for themselves, tearing the bowels and the hearts of the victims. The wounds were seared with burning coals, or molten lard was poured into them. . . . He had invented even more horrible torments, and he inflicted them in cold blood; cannibals would be disgraced by his cruelty; decency forbids us to say more." (*Abrége de l'Hist. de la Hollande.* Kerroux, t. II., p. 310.)*

* The following episode, in the history of persecutions is much apropos of what is written in the text. It relates the passion of the MARTYRS OF GORCUM, who were elevated to the honor of the altars on the occasion of the late Centenary Festival in Rome, June, 1857. It has been translated from the Dutch by the Rev. Joseph De Vries of Bowling Green, Ky., and published in the "New York Freeman's Journal," from whose columns we beg leave to transfer an abridgment to our pages:—

"William van Lumey, a nobleman of Liege, Duke of Mark, and Stadtholder of Holland, was, for his insatiable cruelty towards the Roman Catholics, deservedly called 'The Hangman of the Inquisition of North Holland.'

"In the commencement of 1572 he was compelled, in consequence of some piratical exploits, which he endeavored to justify as blows against the Spanish power, to withdraw his vessels for safety to England.

"He was not, however, allowed to enjoy long this place of

Protestant tolerance of England, France, and Netherlands, finds its counterpart in Sweden.

refuge, as he received positive orders from Queen Elizabeth to leave her kingdom with the fleet, which he commanded as Admiral of the Prince of Orange. Not knowing in what direction he should sail, he was advised by William Blois, of Treslong, who had recently joined him with two vessels, and by Jacob Simonson de Ryk, and other captains of the fleet, to attempt a feat more worthy of their cause. They proposed to sail for Enkhuizen or some other city of North Holland. Lumey was reluctantly forced to yield to their wishes. He set sail in March, in the direction of Texel, with the purpose of attacking the Spanish fleet. Head winds, however, frustrated his design, and he was compelled to run up the river Meuse, with the hope of securing to himself the city of Brielle. As a precaution he sent forward two vessels, under the command of Marinus Brandt and Damian van Haren, which he soon followed with his whole fleet of twenty-four sail. Arrived before the city, he demanded its surrender 'in the name of the Prince of Orange, as Stadtholder of the King of Spain.'

"The town was without garrison, and the authorities, unable to offer resistance, made no reply. Treslong, impatient of delay, forced the south, — whilst Lumey ordered Captain Roobol to burst open the north gate. Both entered the city on the same evening at the head of two hundred and fifty men.

"This daring feat, which we may regard as the groundwork of the independence of Holland, was consummated by Lumey, in a manner worthy of him, since early on the following morning he issued his order to rob and desecrate all the churches and monasteries of the city. It was not without great difficulty that Captains Treslong, Entes, de Ryk and Dirk Duivel prevented Lumey's design of first plundering the whole town and then abandoning it. Thus it was that a roving band of adventurers, who had assumed the contemptible name of Water Geux, made the first successful resistance to the Spanish

There, also, the Reformation was introduced by violence and bloodshed; the religious laws of tyranny, although they most probably did not suspect the great results of this daring attempt.

"From this point Lumey's savage soldiers issued forth into the surrounding country.

"On the 25th of June, 1572, at about 8, A. M., which was the day following the surrender of Dordrecht, Marinus Brandt appeared before Gorcum and demanded the surrender of the city. The citizens, many of whom were tainted with the new heresies, being much divided, the city went over on the 26th. But the commander, Gaspar Turk, unable to resist the excited populace, withdrew to the Castle, offering to all that would follow him a secure asylum until his son, William Turk, should arrive with the necessary reinforcements. He also encouraged those of the Catholics who had followed him with a letter of the Spanish commander-in-chief, Duke Bossu, who promised him assistance.

"Amongst his followers were Father Nicholas Pieck, Guardian of the Franciscan Monastery of Gorcum, and sixteen of his brethren, who had carried with them the sacred vestments and Church ornaments. Three others refused to accompany them, and remained in the monastery. Leonardus Van Vegchel and Nicholas Poppel, two of the city pastors, returned to the town to warn the people and to urge the Catholics to take refuge within the castle.

"Brandt, having entered the city at the head of his Geux, commanded the citizens to assemble on the market-place, where he made them take the oath of allegiance, which pledged them to be faithful to the king and the Royal Commander of the Netherlands, — William of Nassau, Prince of Orange; to resist the Duke of Alba, and to defend the new evangelical doctrine. He next ordered them to shout, 'Long live the Geux,'" to which Turk from his castle played an accompani-

that country have preserved as much of their cruel enactments as the spirit of the times will

ment, by the discharge of two cannons among the Geux. Brandt, perceiving that the commander was in earnest, sent to him a letter by one of the Franciscans who had remained in the city, which Turk would not receive. The messenger, however, read the letter, — which promised the commander and all his followers leave to retire, free and unmolested. He refused. Brandt prepared immediately to storm the fort, and commenced operations that very evening. Turk bravely defended the post with which he was entrusted, although he had but twenty soldiers at his disposal. The Geux soon gained the outworks. He then retreated to that part of the castle which was called the Blue Tower. The first loss, however, had so discouraged his little band, that now they threw away their arms and refused to obey. At this juncture, Brandt demanded anew the surrender of the fort, promising, on his oath, that all, lay and clerical, might go without hindrance, only they were required to leave behind them whatever treasure they had concealed within the castle. Turk hesitated until midnight, when, seeing no signs of relief, he surrendered to the Geux on the 27th June. When the clergy learned the news, knowing that they would certainly be recognized from their dress, they made their confession, and received the Holy Communion at the hands of Father Nicholas.

"Upon entering the fort, Brandt gave his hand to Hesselius Estius, who was standing at the entrance, saying: 'Fear not; what I have promised I promise again, and pledge by my oath.' Scarcely, however, had the savage horde entered, when the prisoners—and above all the ecclesiastics—experienced the roughest treatment. The Geux forthwith assailed them, and searched their pockets and clothes for money. The vice-guardian, a venerable old man whom they took to be the guardian, had to suffer much. They grabbed him by the

allow. Not long ago (in 1861) six whole families were banished the country, their goods

breast, and abused him violently to force him to give up the money, which the holy man, faithful to the rule of his order, did not have.

"After the list of the prisoners was made out, Brandt reproached Gaspar Turk with the death of two citizens, whom he had beheaded for lodging and patronizing heretical preachers. Turk replied that he had done what his office obliged him to do.

"But from this moment the Geux began in earnest their insults and outrages upon the ecclesiastics, who bore it with admirable patience. A citizen of Gorcum offered to ransom the guardian, who was his relative; but the noble Nicholas Pieck refused positively to abandon his brethren, to whom he ever addressed words of encouragement and confidence. A similar offer was made to the steward of the monastery; he, however, did not hesitate a moment to accept it; he even remained in the castle as the steward of the Geux.

"Being bitterly upbraided with the violation of his word and his oath, Brandt defended himself by saying that he could do nothing further without the orders of Lumey. Yet a few days afterwards the prisoners, with the exception of the ecclesiastics, were ransomed by the concerted action of some citizens. One Catholic alone was excepted with the clerical body; but he also, at the continued instances of his wife, was allowed to go, and with him a certain priest named Godefridus Van Duynen, who was somewhat feeble-minded. But when he was leaving the prison, one of the Geux soldiers remarked, 'If this fellow has sense enough to serve God, he must have sense enough to be hanged.' Whereupon he was returned to the prison, and afterwards actually martyred with the others.

"After the citizens were dismissed, the guardian was thrown, with all his companions, into a subterranean dungeon, in which both pastors of the city, with one other priest, had been

confiscated, only because they had entered the Catholic Church. In Norway, Denmark, Prus-

already confined. They were greatly wearied with the ill-treatment and insult which they had received, and they felt also keenly the cravings of hunger. As it was Friday, a day of abstinence, they were served with meat; but they refused to partake of it, notwithstanding the intensity of their appetite. One only, a priest, forgot himself, and ate of the proffered food.

"Some time after, the soldiers, by means of a ladder, came pouring into the prison of the frightened clergy, crying aloud, 'Let us cut off the ears and noses of these idolators and crucify them.' They were about to take off every stitch of their clothes to tie them on the ladder for the purpose of scourging them, when one of the soldiers came in with the tidings that William Turk was approaching with a band of Spanish troops. They hastened to the wall to resist the coming forces; but, failing to see them, they soon left the fortifications to return to the prisoners, who now expected nothing else but to be put to death, one after another. Leonardus therefore walked resolutely up to them and knelt down, saying, 'I am ready,' at the same time uncovering his head and neck. They required him to discover to them the treasures of the monastery. He remained silent. They next fell upon Godefridus; but finding that they could effect nothing with this feeble-minded individual, they turned to Nicholas Goppel, the younger pastor, and put a cocked pistol to his mouth to compel him to point out the hidden treasures. These threats did not in the least disconcert him. They then seized the cincture of a Franciscan brother, threw it around Poppel's neck, and dragged him to the door, where they pulled him up and down till he was almost strangled. When he was all but dead, they renewed their demand. Obtaining no information—for how could they, since he knew nothing about it?—they

sia, and Geneva, wherever it reigns, Protestantism had ever proved itself the sworn enemy and

kicked him aside, thinking that he was dead. At the time of his death the marks of the cord were still plainly visible.

"Now they went again at the Franciscans, inflicting all sorts of tortures upon them, especially the younger ones, whose teeth were knocked out. One of the brothers receiving the same abuse, said, 'I know nothing about the hidden treasures; that is the guardian's concern.' 'Who then,' they asked, 'is the head of the traitors?' and with this they seized on Hieronimus, the vicar, whom they conjectured to be the guardian. They put a dagger to his breast and renewed their threats. With one word the vicar could have warded off all danger from himself; but he remained silent and awaited death patiently. Afterwards they discovered the guardian and assailed him furiously. His calm reply was: 'The consecrated chalices and the ornaments were taken into the castle, as you well know; and I am sure that you will not fail to find them!' They heeded not his word, but drew his cincture also up to his neck, dragged him to the door, and repeated on him the torture which they had inflicted on Poppel. The constant friction of the cord, as it passed over the sharp edges of the door, caused it to break, and the holy martyr fell apparently lifeless on the stone floor of the dungeon.

"The savages approached him to ascertain whether he was dead, and placed him in a sitting position against the wall. Not discovering any evidence of life, they held a burning candle to his forehead, burned his hair, blackened his face, mouth, cheeks, chin, and nose. Then they held the flame to his nostrils to make it penetrate to the brain. Their cruelty being not yet satiated, they forced open his mouth and held the burning candle in it, which so burned his tongue and palate as to deprive him of all taste until the end of his martyrdom.

"Not finding any tokens of life in him after these barba-

blind hater of Catholics. Free and unchecked, it spurns all outward regards, which have often

rous tortures, they kicked him aside, saying, 'It was but a monk.' When he came to himself he uttered not a word of complaint in regard to his indescribable sufferings; he only exhorted his brethren to persevere through all their trials.

"The torturers soon returned, armed with a hatchet to hew him to pieces; perceiving, however, that he was still alive, they trampled on his body and breast, exclaiming, 'Does that monk live yet?' Once more they repeated their insults, kicked him and trampled upon him, and then left the dungeon amidst the most horrible imprecations.

"On the following morning the Geux soldiers returned to the prison of the ecclesiastics, and one of them dealt out such heavy blows upon their jaws that the blood streamed out copiously through nose and mouth. Such scenes were often repeated, mostly during the night. Sometimes they were accompanied by invited guests, among others a Walon, whom one of the Franciscans recognized as his countryman, and endeavored to move to pity and commiseration; but, for a reply the latter took a knife and cut his face, so that streams of blood poured from it, adding, 'I will hang you because you are my countryman!'

"The soldiers, too, knelt down before those ecclesiastics, who were priests, as if they wished to confess, and whispered all kinds of vulgar language into their ears, which they followed up with blows and kicks. Willehadus, a superannuated monk, replied to every blow by saying, 'Thanks be to God!' and when one of the Geux inquired 'What he had to say to his confession,' the pious old man said, 'I will pray to God for you.' The Geux struck him for this so violently that he fell fainting to the ground.

"On the 3d of June, the third day of their captivity, Theodore Bommer and Arnold de Koning, both citizens of Gorcum,

given it an appearance of moderation; openly and haughtily it claims what it wills.

were hanged; the first because he had called the Geux, as they passed by him, church robbers; the other for having, in the surrounding country, enlisted soldiers in the name of the king. Brandt had permitted Father Leonardus to assist them in their last moments: at the solicitation of the citizens, he was even allowed to remain in the town on condition that he would be 'liberal' in his preaching. He succeeded, also, with the aid of the nephew of the guardian, in obtaining for him a physician to tend his wounds. When the doctor beheld the barbarous cruelty which he had endured, he could not restrain his tears, and he resolved to visit them daily.

"On the 1st of July, there appeared in the prison a certain John Omalius, a renegade canon of the Church of Liege, who was at present in the service of Lumey. He informed them, amidst the most frightful invectives, that he was deputed by the Duke of Mark to hang all of them. The vicar promptly replied, 'Do with us as you please, — we ask for no delay;' which was answered by Omalius with another volley of abuse.

"On the same day they were visited by a hangman, who showed them the ropes, saying, 'Look what I have got here!' 'Thanks be to God,' quoth the guardian, 'that we have got so far.' He proceeded to tear the cowls from their habits, which he took with him, but the hanging was not yet carried into effect.

"Again during the night, a lot of drunken soldiers rushed in upon the martyrs. After tying them two by two, they put them in a row, yelling, 'Sing now, ye monks, you shall march to death in procession.' They readily went out to the walls of the fort, chanting the *Te Deum*. Here they found a number of Geux soldiers seated at a well-supplied table, who handed them a dice-box, telling them that they might throw

At the Protestant Synod of Breme, Parson Sander, of Ebberfeld, alluding to the Jesuits and to

to see who should be hanged first. 'The throwing of the dice is altogether superfluous,' exclaimed Nicholas Pieck; 'I offer myself as the first victim.'

"After a few more insults and indignities, they were this time led back to the dungeon without any new torture.

"On the following day, the feast of the Visitation of the B. V., Father Leonardus ascended the pulpit of the parochial church. Those who had flocked thither to hear him carry out his promise of preaching 'liberal' sermons, were sadly disappointed; for he boldly preached the pure and unadulterated doctrine, in opposition to all heretical innovations. After this they exerted their utmost to imprison him anew, and made frequent attempts upon his life; the Catholics, however, protected him faithfully. His efforts to effect the ransom of his colleague, Nicholas Poppel, proved abortive, and he himself was finally banished from the city for his bold preaching. When he was leaving the town, the soldiers held on to him, and when a few citizens made an attempt to release him, the Geux shouted that he was a traitor, who was leaving the city without a pass. This was false, for he had obtained a written pass, which these very soldiers had secretly abstracted. Not having anything to show, he was proclaimed a traitor and led back to prison. Marinus Brandt ordered him instantly to be undressed and to be put to the torture, which order, for some unknown reason, he recalled before it could be enforced. He was, however, cast into the dungeon under the pretence of being suspected of treasonable intentions. When he entered, he asked pardon of his former companions in so far as his conduct might have aggravated their condition. The physician, Theodore, was in the mean time the only one who was faithful to them in their misfortunes, carefully treating their wounds and frequently exhorting the guardian to consent to the ransom that was offered

the Pope, exclaims, "Where Protestants have the power, they should not be allowed to *exist*, much less to be free.'

for him, but he persistently refused, saying, 'That the shepherd should not forsake his sheep.'

"Some influential advisers had been active in exerting themselves for the liberation of the captives, and now despatched for this end a message to the Prince of Orange. The Geux, learning this, urged the cruel Lumey, who still remained in Brielle, to have them executed before the reply of the Prince could arrive.

"Lumey had sometime before sent the Lieutenant Omalius to look after the prisoners, and thence to proceed to Bommel, before which city he met with a complete defeat. The news of this disaster embittered Lumey yet more against the captives, and, arrogating to exercise absolute power in the absence of the prince, he ordered their execution. Omalius returned on the 3d of July, from his defeat before Bommel. A few zealous Catholics resolved to try to purchase the freedom of the poor monks from the brute, but they were falsely advised not to make the attempt, since he was, they said, not to be prevailed upon, — not even with gold.

"Not judging it prudent to carry out the execution publicly in Gorcum, he had them taken to the river Merwede on the night of the 6th of July, after robbing them of a portion of their clothing. Those who asked to be allowed to retain their cloaks received in reply heavy blows upon their jaws. At 1, A. M., they were ordered to step into a small boat, which was to take them to Brielle. The master of the craft was a citizen of Gorcum. Leonardus recognized him and said:—

"'Well, Rochus, so you are the man who must take us to the gallows?'

"'Yes,' he replied, 'I have to do it.'

"The boat contained nineteen prisoners, — sixteen priests,

At Geneva, jealous of Catholic growth, the Protestants have formed a covenant, not to buy anything of Catholics, never to employ

and three lay brothers of the Franciscan Monastery. Their number had been reduced occasionally, but circumstances had, from time to time, filled up the vacancies.

"After descending the river some distance, they were transferred to an oyster craft, in which they were closely huddled together, and the repulsive exhalations of which well-nigh stifled them. Nicasius fortunately had some spirits, which the physician had given to him while yet in prison. This he distributed among his brethren, which had the effect of somewhat reviving them. Their stay, however, in this disgusting craft, was but of short duration, as they were soon taken aboard a merchantman, which took them to Dordrecht, where they arrived on the following morning at 9 o'clock. Here they were relieved of some more of their clothing.

"While they were anchored near the wall, curiosity drew multitudes from the city to see them, and looked at them as if they were a collection of wild beasts. They were, moreover, left without food the entire day. The insulting crowd kept increasing to such an extent that they were glad to be allowed to get aboard the vessel upon paying a fee to the soldiers who guarded the prisoners. About noon the tide rose, and Omallus gave orders to sail for Brielle. The Captain managed to give them something to eat, adding, 'I do not know a human being who will not give me a piece of bread in return for this act of kindness.'

"The vessel anchored within three miles of its destination. Throughout the entire night they were left a prey to hunger and cold until, finally, at daybreak, they reached Brielle. They were delayed a whole hour before the gate, till Lumey himself arrived, surrounded by an armed retinue, to give orders for its opening. The barbarian eyed them for a long

them, to reduce them to want, to see that Protestants alone are raised to offices and places.

time with a grinning smile. 'What do you come here for? Have you come hither to ply your treachery and upset our plans? You had better remain at home to read your masses!' Such was his greeting. He then commanded his soldiers to lead them forth from the vessel, and to compel them to kneel down before him, whilst he addressed them the Latin words, '*Surgite, Domini!*'—'Gentlemen, arise!' Being tied two and two, they put a blazed standard, which they had stolen from one of the churches, into the hands of the lay brother Henry, and made him march on before his companions. Three times they had to pass in this manner under the gallows 'in order,' as the soldiers expressed themselves, 'to fulfil the vow of their pilgrimage.' The populace, in the mean time, assailed them with a torrent of ridicule and insult, pointing to them the gallows as they yelled, 'Look, there is your church and your graveyard.' They were ordered now to kneel down under the gallows and to chant the Litanies of the Saints and of the Blessed Virgin, while the hangman seemed to prepare himself for his work; for these preparations were only made to frighten them. The hangman finally snatched the standard from the hands of Henry, and placed himself at the head of the procession. Soldiers and people drove them on with clubs, Lumey himself striking them in the face with the limb of a tree. They were marched to the market-place, where, in the same manner as outside the gate, they were placed under the gallows. Here they were commanded to recite aloud the Litanies of the Saints and of the Blessed Virgin, which were answered by the crowd with mockery and ridicule. At the close of these insults they were removed to prison, where two other priests were already incarcerated,—Andrew Wouters, pastor of Heinoort, and Adrian, pastor of Maasdam. Thirty minutes later two other monks were added. After occupying

And all this by men who, in terms of indignation, demand liberty and equality of worship,

this damp subterranean dungeon until three in the evening, they were led to the court-house, where Lumey, assisted by a few chosen persons, proposed to them some questions concerning their faith, which were all thoroughly answered by Leonardus. They were remanded to their dungeon; only the pastor of Maasdam, the canon of Gorcum, and the lay brother Henry were put in a better prison and served with bread and water, probably because they had answered their interrogators more satisfactorily.

"On the following day, 7th of July, seven of them were examined anew and solicited to abjure their faith. The leader of these so-called judges was a seaman called Cornelius, who, finding that he could not unsettle their belief, vociferated incessantly, ' Let them be hanged !' They were returned again to prison. In the mean time the Catholics of Gorcum had received, from the Prince of Orange, a letter of protection for the prisoners. It was addressed to Marinus Brandt, who gave a copy of it to a prominent and zealous Catholic. On the following day the City Council of Gorcum sent a messenger to Lumey, with a copy of the order for the release of the prisoners. But Lumey protested that he ' considered himself as much at the head of the Republic as the prince, and that he did not expect to receive orders from anybody, — he cared not whom. As regarded the prisoners, upon these he would revenge the death of Dukes Egmond and Hoorne, and many others; this was decreed and determined irrevocably.' Much as Treslong and some other captains pleaded in their favor and insisted on their liberation, Lumey and his party prevailed.

"The order of the Prince of Orange had deeply wounded the pride of this infamous officer, and only served to fire his fury against him and the ecclesiastics. He had promised, too, the feast of their execution to the people of Brielle, and he would

even where they are a small minority; by men who perpetually boast of liberty of con-

not deprive them of this pleasure. Neither prayers nor gold could avail, and the messenger returned to Gorcum without effecting anything, to the great astonishment of all those who were interested in them.

"The guardian, Nicholas Pieck, was again, on the following day, cited before a tribunal which offered to set him free with all his companions, if only they would forswear the Pope of Rome. This proposition was purposely made to him, because they thought that his example would easily induce the others to follow. But he refused most emphatically. A supper was now offered them, probably to weaken thereby their minds, but all agreed with the guardian, who told the judges 'that he would never abandon his brethren and companions in life or in death; nor would he do anything to weaken their faith in any point; that all had resolved rather to meet death than to deny one tenet of their religion.'

"Lumey, learning their determination, passed immediately upon them the sentence of death. At 11, P. M., the martyrs were roused from their sleep, and notified that the hour of their execution had struck. 'What the Lord has given,' replied Father Nicholas, ' I cannot refuse.'

"The prisoners were again tied as before, and led outside the gate amidst a great concourse of people, who heaped upon them all possible mockery and insult. Here they were again joined by the lay brother, Henry, who had been separated from them on a previous occasion, for having probably denied some doctrine of the faith. He manifested the most profound grief, and ardently wished to share their martyrdom. His companions welcomed him back, which again increased their number to twenty-one. The martyrs were conducted to a place where an Augustinian monastery used to stand, dedicated to St. Elizabeth. The monks had deserted it before it was de-science, Christian charity, and of a religion of peace and love; by men who profess to believe

molished by the Geux. A large barn, which had been used to stow away turf, was still standing. It had two cross-beams, which were considered very suitable for the hanging of the martyrs. As soon as they were brought in, they confessed, and recommended their souls to God. The guardian was selected as the first victim. He embraced his brethren, and admonished and begged them to persevere courageously until death in this struggle for their faith. He then ascended the ladder lightly and without hesitation, continuing his exhortations till the rope closed around his neck. When the voice of the venerable guardian was hushed, the noble Hieronimus and Nicholas Poppel took up the word, and encouraged their brethren to persevere until the end; for a Calvinist preacher exerted his utmost, especially with the younger ones, to induce them to renounce their faith, by promising them life and distinguished consideration for their apostasy. His words, however, produced no effect except on the youngest novice, Henry, who did all that was asked of him to preserve his life. His youth may be alleged as some excuse, since he was only eighteen years of age, and the fear of death crushed out of him all other sentiments.

"The vicar Hieronimus behaved with great courage. While ascending the ladder, he said to the preacher, who pretended to speak to him words of comfort: '*It is no hardship for me to die; but it is painful to witness that an inexperienced youth has heeded your words.*' This reply made the soldiers furious; they attacked anew the old defenceless clergyman, and drew their knives through his face, so that it became horribly disfigured. Their barbarity carried them so far that, after he had been suspended, they cut out from the flesh the cross, which, agreeable to a regulation of his order, he wore on his breast and right arm. He was succeeded by Nicasius and the pastor Nicholas. Before

in Jesus Christ, and with whom one is perfectly free to be an infidel, a Pantheist, an Atheist, but not a Catholic!

VI. CATHOLIC INTOLERANCE. — We know now what to think of the vaunted tolerance of Protestants. Let us examine on what ground

their death, they addressed a few words in Latin to their remaining companions, which, however, were not understood by the novice, Henry, who was not, as yet, sufficiently conversant with that language, and to whom we owe in great part the particulars of this history.

"A Franciscan, whose name was William, spoke a few words to the Walon soldiers, who surrounded him and whose countryman he was. They cut the ropes with which he was bound, and removed him. He had renounced the faith and forfeited the crown of martyrdom.

"Godefridus van Mervel, the sacristan, whose office it was to keep the consecrated vessels, retained the secret of their hiding-place till the end, and when climbing the ladder repeated the words of our Saviour, 'Lord, forgive them, for they know not what they do.' Leonardus, being led to death, exhorted his brethren, and said, 'I regret not that I am going to die a death which is truly desirable, but I leave behind me a mother and a sister, for whom nature prompts me to feel, for I know that the news of my death will greatly afflict them.'

"It was next the turn of Godefridus van Duynen, who, as has been stated before, was somewhat feeble-minded. Stepping upon the ladder, he said to his executioners, 'Hurry on, I pray you, that I may join my brethren. If I have any way offended any of you, I beg you, for the love of God, to forgive me.' Then he was hanged, and he breathed his last.

"We add the names of the above martyrs, — eleven of whom

the hackneyed charge of intolerance is made against the Catholics. This charge contains both a truth and a falsehood.

The Church is certainly intolerant in matters of doctrine. True; and we glory in it! Truth is of itself intolerant. In religion, as in mathematics, what is true, is true, and what is false is false. No compromise between truth and error; truth cannot compromise. Such concessions, however small, would prove an immediate destruction of truth. Two and two make four: it

were Franciscans; the other eight belonged also to religious communities."

  NICHOLAS PIECK,
  HIERONIMUS VAN WEERT,
  THEODORUS VAN EMBDEM,
  NICASIUS JANSSEN VAN HEEZE,
  WILLEHADUS DANUS,
  GODEFRIDUS VAN MERVEL,
  ANTONIUS VAN WEERT,
  ANTONIUS VAN HORNAAR,
  FRANCISCUS ROY,
  PETRUS VAN ASSCHE,
  CORNELIUS VAN WYK,
  LEONARDUS VAN VEGCHEL,
  NICHOLAS POPPEL,
  GODEFRIDUS VAN DUYNEU,
  JOANNES VOSTERWYK,
  JOANNES (Priest of the Order of Preachers),
  ADRIAN VAN BEEK,
  JACOBUS LACOPS,
  ANDREAS WOUTERS.

is a *truth*. Hence whoever asserts the contrary, utters a falsehood. Let it be an error of a thousandth or of a millionth part, it will ever be false to assert that two and two do *not* make four.

The Church proclaims and maintains truths as certain as the mathematical ones. She teaches and defends truths with as much intolerance as the science of mathematics defends hers. And what more logical? The Catholic Church alone, in the midst of so many different sects, avers a possession of absolute truth, out of which there cannot be true Christianity; she alone has a right to be, she alone must be, intolerant. She alone will and must say, as she has said through all ages, in her councils: "*If any one saith or believeth contrary to what I teach, which is truth*, LET HIM BE ANATHEMA!"

At the same time, our Lord, intrusting her with the deposit of truth, has also left in her his spirit of charity and patience. Intolerant as regards the doctrine, the Church has mercy for the people, and never has she had recourse to lawful measures of rigor, but after all manner of kindness and persuasion have failed.

She has visited only the incorrigible, and then as a last resort. She was constrained to do so, to preserve from contagion the souls of the faithful, to put an end to scandals, and to fulfil those great duties of a justice — not less divine than mercy is.

In her patience and in her tolerance towards persons as well as in her intolerance for what concerns doctrine, the Catholic Church faithfully follows in the footsteps of her Chief and her GOD, our Lord JESUS CHRIST, who is truth, mercy, and justice.

As for those anti-Catholic historians who write so much about the pretended barbarism of the Church in the middle ages, their misrepresentations are entirely discredited by the conscientious labors of a new generation of historians far more impartial than their predecessors. "To live, Protestantism found itself forced to build up a history of its own," said the celebrated historian Thierry,—certainly not suspected of any partiality towards the Church.

There are Protestants now, who, divesting themselves of all party spirit, protest against those old slanders, criminal exaggerations, and perfidious insinuations, with which old histories are crammed. "For the last three centuries," says de Maistre, " history has been a permanent conspiracy against truth."

VII. THE INQUISITION, ST. BARTHOLOMEW, AND THE DRAGONNADES OF THE CEVENNES. — A few words more about Catholic intolerance. Protestants never tire of casting up against the Catholics certain facts, which they allege as proofs to convince them of intolerance, — the *Inquisition*, *St. Bartholomew*, and the *Dragonnades of the Cévennes*.

These items have furnished materials for romances and plays; but writers of novelettes and plays do not profess regard for historical accuracy, and people of common sense and seekers of truth do not generally look to them for information.

1. What is, then, this *Inquisition*, which frightens us so much, even in these, our days? Popular romances represent it as a terrible tribunal, raised in every Catholic land, torturing poor victims in deep dungeons, and burning them at the stake, with surrounding fires never put out.

The Protestant historians, Ranke and Guizot, honorably admit that the Spanish Inquisition was only a political institution to protect the unity of Spain. The rulers of that kingdom looked upon heresy as the enemy most dangerous to the peace of their dominions, and declared it a crime of high treason against the nation. Unable to decide by themselves, or their civil courts, questions of faith, they established an ecclesiastic tribunal, charged with the examination of prisoners and with judgment on their orthodoxy. The inquisitors then acquainted the prince with the result of their examination, and the latter pronounced sentence as he deemed best.

That institution you may value as you choose; you are at liberty to condemn the abuses and the cruelties of which it has been guilty through the violence of political passions and the character of the Spaniard; yet one cannot but acknowledge, in the terrible part taken by the clergy in its trials, the most legitimate and most natural exercise of ecclesiastical authority. Does not the examination of questions of faith belong by right divine to the Church? but what man of good faith will ever confound these acts, exclusively religious, with the office of the executioner?

But remember that the Popes have never ceased to protest against the rigors of the Spanish Inquisition, although it received no prestige whatever from their authority, it being, as we have seen, a political institution of the Spanish kingdom.

2. But you will say, "What of the Saint

Bartholomew?—that frightful massacre ordered by the Church, to the sacrifice of so many Protestant lives?"

The Saint Bartholomew, even more than the Inquisition of Spain, is a political event.* Protestants rebelled against lawful authority; they had attempted to seize the person of the king, and endeavored to establish in the midst of the nation a people turbulent and revolutionary. The youthful Charles IX. and the haughty Catharine Medici, his mother, were threatened in their lives and liberty by the conspiracy of Amboise; they had to fly for their lives before that of Meaux. The leaders of the Protestant party grew more insolent every day. The queen, thus goaded, resolved to get rid of the rebels, and called to her assistance the religious excitement fanned into frenzy by the

---

* In the "North British Review," June, 1863, we read: "One word as to the massacre. The difficulties experienced even in these days in arriving at the truth should suggest that some allowance should be made for the attitude taken up by the Pope. *Te Deum*, medals, and frescoes, in celebration of a massacre, are not in themselves things well fitted to soften Protestant prejudices. But we must bear in mind that upon this, as upon other momentary occasions, the See of Rome was imperatively called upon for immediate action, before the true facts of the case could by any possibility have been really known, IF, INDEED, THEY WERE NOT DESIGNEDLY CONCEALED."

fury of the Huguenots. Religion was the *pretext*, but not the cause of the Saint Bartholomew. Men well read in history know it to be so in these our days; why, then, do not Protestant historians acknowledge it in good faith?

"Very well," you urge; "but did not the Pope sing a *Te Deum* on the occasion of that butchery?" Yes, he did; but Gregory XIII. had been deceived as to the facts. He received a hurried despatch from the French court, that a murderous attempt had been made on the lives of the king and of his family, and that they had been delivered from the hands of the Huguenots, and the assassins had been punished; whereupon the Pope went to St. Peter's and returned public thanks to GOD. He did not know the lamentable truth of that night. Those excesses have, however, been greatly exaggerated by the party; for after all the *Protestant* martyrology could not set down the number of victims, all counted, but at seven hundred and eighty-six, for all France. Because those men, in rebellion against their sovereign, had been shot down as turbulent Calvinists, is it a reason why the Catholic Church should be held accountable for their death? The whole blame of the Saint Bartholomew is therefore laid, and solely, on the machiavellian conduct of Charles IX. and of his mother.

Without any purpose of excusing that which cannot be excused, we must observe that men and institutions always bear the stamp of the times. In those ages, public manners were rude and uncouth, and their character affected men and things, good and evil. Moreover the religious sentiment had a mastery over all the rest. Accordingly, Protestant violence came into collision with an excitability of faith whereof we have no idea. To it we must refer, for the most, the extreme measures which accompanied many historical facts of those days.

3. Although this asperity of manners was somewhat softened in France in the days of Louis XIV., it yet was the cause of lamentable results at the time of the revocation of the Edict of Nantes. I shall not canvass here the nature of that act of Louis. But truth compels us to remember that, during the cruelties practised against the Huguenots in certain parts of the Cévennes, the king's officers went beyond the orders of their master, and they alone were guilty. Irritated at the attempt made by the Protestants to sunder the unity of the nation, to plot with strangers, to hold continued practice with England, Louis XIV. resolved upon purging

France of this leaven of discord. To assert the rights of the crown, as well as those of religion, he called force to his assistance. But it is well known how Bossuet and Fenelon, however of one mind with the king, deprecated those cruel and violent measures. What, then, in the presence of these simple facts, becomes of the charges preferred by the enemies of the faith? And how can the *dragonnades* of the Cévennes be turned into an argument against the Church?

Here we have three facts, three political crimes, if you will, for which Protestants make the Church responsible after three hundred years. Oh! but St. Francis de Sales spoke well when, at the utterance of so many slanders against the Church by the Protestants of his own time, he compared her to the chaste Susanna, falsely accused by those men who should have been her defenders! That sainted woman, brought to the pillory, exclaimed:—

"O Eternal God, who knowest hidden things! . . . Thou knowest that they have borne false witness against me; whereas, I have done none of these things which these men have maliciously forged against me."

"And the Lord raised the spirit of young Daniel, and he cried out with a loud voice:—

"' Are ye so foolish, ye children of Israel, that, without examination or knowledge of the truth, ye have condemned a daughter of Israel?'

" And the people rose and did justice to the innocence and sanctity of the chaste Susanna." (Dan. xiii.)

VIII. PROTESTANT MARTYRS. — PROTESTANTISM HAS NO MARTYRS. — A *martyr* gives his life in steadfast testimony of the faith of *Jesus Christ*. He dies, not for the sake of personal opinion, but for the doctrine of the Church of GOD. He is not *obstinate* but *faithful*. Hence every Christian put to death out of hatred to the faith is a martyr.

Are those few Protestants, who have suffered martyrdom for their religious opinions, martyrs? Not at all. They staked their lives to uphold private ideas and convictions purely human; preferring their own defiance to their lives. It is a death crowning man's pride; whereas, a veritable martyrdom is the most perfect act of humble submission and total self-abnegation. It is not enough to be killed in order to be a martyr. It must needs be a death suffered for the sake of a truth which one's honor will maintain even at the cost of life.

In the pretended martyrs of reformed

sects we find fanaticism, defiance, self-glory, and madness, — all offspring of pride. On the other hand, the true martyrs — those whom Holy Church offers to Jesus Christ, from St. Stephen down to those recently killed for the faith in China and Ava — all die in the peace of God; meek and humble, like innocent victims, expressing love for their executioners, — martyrs worthy of Jesus both in life and death.

IX. An Instance of Protestant Moderation. — We often hear Protestants complaining of the violent style of Catholic writers. It is a clerical ruse of great and keen cunning; because, on the other hand, they vaunt great moderation and tenderness in their attitude towards the Church.

Now, we have something to say about it: —

1. What they are pleased to call violence in Catholic writers is only an ardent zeal for the truth, — that zeal which devoured our Saviour, Jesus Christ, when he whipped the buyers and sellers out of the temple, and made Pharisees and scribes writhe under his scathing anathemas.

2. Catholics attack Protestantism, but only on the *defensive*, against Protestants. Protestantism is a rebellion, essentially unwarrantable,

against truth and the Church, and the children of the Church and of truth never take up arms against Protestantism but to ward off its attacks and save their faith.

3. Lastly, this Protestant moderation is of a kind both with their style of controversy and their tolerance. It does *not* exist, and we defiantly hurl back the charge they advance against us.

We shall now give a proof of a general character,—a well-known proof,—upheld alike by the Protestant and the socialistic press.

The journals of the principal sects of France —*Le Lien, L'Esperance, Les Archives*—have with great zeal announced and encouraged a book as one of the very best, and one which is to be found in all the Protestant publishing houses of Paris. It is an old work by the Lutheran, Marnix de Sainte-Aldegonde recently re-ushered before the public, with a preface by Mr. Quinet.

No Protestant organ protests against its republication. Nay; *all* hail its appearance.

The preface says: "Our work is not only to refute Popery, but to *root it out;* not to root it out only, but to *brand it with infamy;* not only to brand it with infamy, but to *stifle it under the mire."* — (p. 7.) "Catholicity must be done away with."

"Whoever undertakes to root out that sickly and mischievous superstition (Catholicity), provided he feels able to do it, should, first of all, remove such superstition out of sight of the people, and render its practice absolutely and physically impossible. At the same time no hope should be held out for its reappearance." — (p. 31.)

"This religious despotism (the Catholic Church) cannot be rooted out unless we get rid of all legality. . . . Blind as it is, it dooms itself to be the victim of *blind force*." (p. 37.)

"No; no truce with THE UNJUST." (p. 42.)

"The principle that all religions are equal is at variance with all philosophy, all science, and all history. . . . There exists a religion which glories in its being incompatible with modern liberties. Had the French Revolution seen this difference plainly, it might, by a concentration of its powers, enmities, and decisions have *exterminated* a worship which denies existence to modern civilization. But . . that revolution was *wanting in audacity*, . . . and the (Catholic) worship, which it was its mission to break, came out of its hands stronger, healthier, and bolder than ever. Let us not be guilty of the same again. — (pp. 57 and fol.)

This is a plain talk. We know where we should find ourselves were Protestantism to triumph over the Christian Church! In the face of such open violence, thus openly exciting people to hatred against, and to the destruction of, religion, who will dare find fault with us Christians because we rise to defend our faith and our life?

However, we should not much wonder at this incredible challenge to persecute and annihilate the Church with fire and sword. Mr. Quinet only repeats, with a faint echo, the sanguinary declamations of the founders of Protestantism. He only writes to-day what Luther and Calvin wrote three hundred years ago, and wrote in terms so exaggerated and with a fury so deep, that the revolutionists of our times could not hold the candle to them.

In his fine work *On Protestantism*, Augustus Nicolas says: "No language did ever lend itself to express the sanguinary violence of Luther's writings. His *The Papacy of Rome Founded by the Devil* is a blot that will disgrace forever not only the literature of Germany, but even the annals of mankind. The Pope" (truly the pen almost refuses to copy the words) "is the devil. Were I able to kill the devil, should I not do it at the peril of my life? The Pope is an enraged wolf, against which the whole world should rise without waiting for a magistrate's warrant. In such matters there can never be cause for regret, unless it were for not having been able to plunge the dagger deeper in his breast. . . . No sooner were the Pope convicted by the Gospel, than the whole world should rush and fall upon him, slaughtering him, and with him his emperors and kings and princes and lords, without mercy. Yes, we should fall upon them with all kinds of weapons, and wash our hands in their blood. . . . Monarchs and princes and lords who belong to the crew of the Roman Sodom should be attacked with all kinds of arms, and we should wash our hands in their blood. . . ." (T. xii. f. 233, seq. — T. i. f. 51, *a*. — T. ix. f. 24, *b*. ed. Wittenb.)

"Shall I mention Calvin, from or on whose pen perpetually flourished the epithets of rascal, drunken sot, raving madman, beast, hog, donkey, dog, etc.? Hear him: "As for the Jesuits, who are our greatest opponents, they should be put to death; or, if that could not be easily done, they should be expelled, or certainly crushed out with lies and calumnies.'"— (pp. 469, 70.)

Just what Quinet advises, — the papacy must be rooted out; it must be dishonored, choked in the mire. After such violent declarations by Luther and Calvin, it is easily understood why the revolutionists of our days have so much sympathy for Protestantism. But it is passing all understanding how such Protestant journals as are called *moderate*, and Protestant publishers, should have advertised and offered for sale the work of Marnix and its preface!

Marnix's book is a tissue of obscenities, of infamies so revolting that respect for my readers and for myself will not allow me to make any quotation from it. I made an attempt, but gave it up in disgust. He utters blasphemies which no Christian should dare repeat, not even for the purpose of inspiring a salutary horror of them. And yet, there you have a Protestant work, republished, after three centuries, in Belgium with the aid of a national subscription of Protestants, infidels, and free masons; and it is sold in noonday light in Paris,—a Catholic city!

Yes, let Protestants wonder at the generous indignation of Catholics! Let them complain because the children of the Church resent and repel the insults heaped on their mother! Let them boast, forsooth, of their *meekness* and of their *moderation*.

"*Questi moderati sono gente di rabbia infinita*," said to me once an Italian priest. They call themselves moderate, but their fury is infinite.

X. OF THOSE PERSECUTIONS WHEREOF PROTESTANTS CLAIM TO HAVE BEEN THE VICTIMS. — Protestants will always persecute when they are the majority; but if they happen to be in the minority they'll whine out doleful tunes of being persecuted. To hear them they are even this day persecuted in France and in Rome, — a charge so strange that we must establish it clearly before we refute it.

Well, then, hear what Mr. Le Savoureux, Protestant minister of Limoges, said at a public meeting in Queen Street, Edinburgh, 1857: "I have good news to give you from motherland (France). The faint light of the Gospel is advancing. Our fathers allowed Protestantism to become extinguished, in spite of the struggle of our *good Huguenots*, but the ancient national churches are getting up. Such nations as France, Spain, etc., under the sway of Rome are *dead nations*. Romanism is the enemy of moral good. The commune of Villefavard has become Protestant; we have *swept the Saints* out of the Church. We have established ten schools in the department of Allier, and, *had we money*, we Protestants would have attained a majority. But since the *coup-d'etat* a man appeared—that Napoleon—who has allied himself with Catholic ideas, has closed our schools, and summoned us before the courts of Justice. *We are now hidden in the woods!* Yet the progress continues. At Limoges *the work* was broken up by a railroad. Had we been Romans the administration would not have disturbed us!" And the Limosin clerk winds up by begging God to grant them *Liberty!*

The Paris correspondent of the "London Times" gives even a more melancholy picture of the heart-rending situation of Protestantism in France. Poor ministers thrown into jail; churches and schools wantonly disbanded.

Hear these *truthful* correspondents: "Yes, we have seen whole populations *taking refuge in forests*, as their fathers did before them, in order to practise their religion. To escape the intrusions of the police they had to keep watchers to warn them in time. Hymns were sung only at intervals, prayers and sermons were broken up, and when the officers arrived they only saw men, women, and children picking up acorns, or climbing up trees." (Times, Jan. 5, 1858.)

It is well known how these ridiculous assertions, so often and so impudently repeated called forth, at last, a rejoinder from the "Moniteur," denying their truth with indignation and contempt. True, not all the Protestants of France push so far the mania of complaining, whether right or wrong; yet the majority among them seem to find a pleasure in calling and believing themselves injured, interfered with in both their rights and their interests, balked in their movements, in a word, *persecuted*. In their writings, in their journals, in their sermons, and above all in the courts of justice, they forever complain of being the victims of persecution.

But what victims, great GOD! Would to Heaven the Catholics of Ireland and Sweden were victims like them! Never was a creed more free and more favored than Protestantism is in France this day. Count them: A late census set their number at *several hundred thousand* in *thirty-six millions* of people. Count the offices they fill from the highest to the lowest. Search the public accounts and compare the pay of Protestant ministers with the compensation given to the Catholic clergy. They are free, not only among their own people but even among the Catholics, to employ the most active propagandism, free to defend themselves and free to attack others. See the relation on which their many temples and schools stand to their number in Paris, *thirteen thousand* — after official reports. Remember, that these schools, increasing every day in number, in the very centre of wards almost exclusively Catholic, are filled for the most with the children of the poor enticed away from the Church. Remember, also, that the works of Marnix de Sainte-Aldegonde (it is enough to quote this work for all) is sold with impunity by all their booksellers. . . Then, lay your hand on your breast, and tell me, reader, can they really call themselves persecuted in France? Indeed, their complaints are unjust, and very awkward in their ingratitude. *

* *Galignani* of Paris, in its issue of Saturday, June 20, 1867, announces for the next day *thirteen* places open to Protestant worship : " Forney's Letters from Europe." Letter xxv. — Phila.: Peterson Bros., 1867. Thus, even in Rome, more liberty is allowed to Protestants than Catholics ever obtained in purely Protestant countries. At what price could a Catholic priest officiate in England under Elizabeth? Could a priest even make his appearance in Geneva when Calvin ruled there ? And was not William Penn called to an account because he allowed a mass-house in Philadelphia ? And did not the

XI. THE MARKET OF SOULS. — Heretical books and pamphlets are spread broadcast all over Catholic countries. Yet this distribution, dangerous and active though it be, is only a secondary means for the agents of the Protestant propaganda. There is still a more powerful agent, to which they are not ashamed to have recourse, — MONEY. Says the Archbishop of Genoa, in one of his pastorals: "A unanimous cry of indignation re-echoes from all parts of Catholic Europe. It would be astonishing indeed, yet a useless effort, were the Protestant so reckless as to deny it."

There is no gainsaying this traffic of consciences. I know very well that there are some

Protestants of Maryland put their heels on the neck of the Catholics, who had been their greatest benefactors, as soon as they got the upper hand? . . . . And so forever. Now look to Rome. Protestants go and come; some of them civil, some very impertinent and insulting. The Pope does not mind them. He even allows them to meet at their ambassadors' houses and have service. Point to such privileges in a thorough Protestant city; and if the Pope does not allow a public meeting-house to be opened in the centre of Rome, nobody can blame him, because, the Pope being the Depository of Divine Truth he cannot conscientiously countenance the manifestations of what is opposed to that truth. Yet he allows them to meet *extra muros*. Rome is the property of the Catholic world, not of Italy, and the Pope of Rome holds it in trust for the Catholic community scattered all over the world.

among the Protestants, laity and clergy, who will never have recourse to such means. They become indignant at such charges made against Protestantism, and I hear with pleasure the energetic disavowal in favor of their individual honor; but it avails nothing against the effort of their propaganda, which endeavors to entice the poor with fat baits of money and temporal gain, in order to make them apostatize. Daily experience places this assertion beyond the possibility of denial. Those who love and help the poor continually meet with such attempts at seduction; yet they are very far from knowing them all. The unfortunates, who allow themselves to be seduced, are on their guard lest their infamy should be known, and sectarian agents limit their reports only to the number of *converts*. Were we able to judge by the number of refusals, the amount of attempts would reach a very high figure. I have myself come across a large number of artisans' families, and distressed families who have received offers of help, work, and gold, sometimes in large sums, *on condition they would turn Protestants*. The venerable parish priest of St. Sulpice, in Paris, on the occasion of an investigation made in his parish, in 1858, laid before the minister of public worship a very lengthy document containing numerous depositions of families and individuals, attesting the criminal intrusions of Protestant propagandism.

"Have you never seen," said an illustrious prelate, not long ago, "some of these dealers in consciences running over the country, walking through our streets, and even worming themselves into the bosom of families to sow their cockle and their lies? It is a new trade amongst us, yet it is spreading alarmingly. Attention should be called to it.

"It happens thus: There is in a village a poor family heavily in debt, and they are about selling their cabin, — their only place of shelter; but there appears one of these soul-brokers who are always on the scent of misfortune. In a tone of perfect good nature he tells the head of the family: 'Poor man! you are badly lodged indeed in this cabin, open to all the winds; how you must suffer from cold! How is it that your priest does not help you to repair your house and to dress yourselves comfortably? . . . Well, I am a Protestant minister, but when I find any poor in my parish I assist them. Come to my house to-morrow and I'll give a warm blanket for your bed, and good clothing for your children.' And off he goes leaving those poor people in an ecstasy of admiration for so much goodness.

"The warm blanket arrives, and the parson does not tarry far behind. This time he talks about repairing the cabin, and he tells them that the requisite sum will be at hand, only that they are not Protestants. At this the woman flares up, and the preacher takes himself off, leaving behind nothing but a bad book.

"Perchance it is a laboring man who falls sick. His wife and children depend on his arms for their support. Poverty and hunger are bad advisers, and often are the source of terrible temptations. Those traders on souls know it; they are on the spot, and offer bread to those wretches, provided they will barter their souls. Alas! they do it.

"Near by, a creditor has seized upon the cot and the little field of a poor countryman, who has nothing else to depend on. The preachers offer him cash enough to rescue his property from the hammer, provided he gives up his Church. With tears he does give it up!

"A poor mother begs a living from door to door, followed by her two little children. The brokers set a couple of their zealous maids after her: they wish to take care of her children and bring them up properly. To compound matters with her conscience, she gives up one, and reserves the other for God.

"These traders drive the best bargains with drunkards, who are forever in want of money. Bankrupts who need a plank, and lewd women who have nothing but a rotten soul to sell, are also good customers: simpletons and dolts afford good chances. No matter where you are, in hotels or taverns, aboard steamboats, in stages, on the highways, you stumble on preachers, catechizers, Bible carriers, who all seem anxious to convert the whole world, each to his own sect." * — (*Du Commerce des Consciences et de l'agitation Protestante en Europe.* Annecy, 1856.)

France, its large cities, Paris, above all, are infested by these indefatigable Protestants. Their chiefs have said: "We must get hold of Paris by all means: once in Paris France is ours: through France we can master Europe." Accordingly paid agents and fanatical women,

---

* What is here written, as European experience, tallies too well with what we see and experience in America. Even this very day (Aug. 27, 1867) a parson, not five miles from my residence, is tampering with the souls of the children of two Catholic families, emboldened by the distance at which they are from their Church and their pastor's residence.

deacons and deaconesses, etc., creep into the dwellings of our poor people and buy them or their children.

The Vicar-General of Lyons, Mr. Cattet, thus writes on this subject:—

" . . . When we were drawing the picture of these shameful practices employed by Protestantism for the purpose of proselytizing, we had an abundance of affidavits of such poor Catholics in country places as had thus been seduced, who, ashamed of themselves and repenting for having sold themselves to the apostles of the *new gospel*, gave us written declarations of the contemptible means of seduction employed against them. Since then we have forwarded to the rector of the Academy of Lyons four affidavits from heads of families, who also declare that they have received money with a pledge that their children should attend Protestant schools.*

"It was a sensible remark, and we love to repeat it, made by one of these bribed wretches who has since recanted in the hands of one of

---

*Should a law be passed in Italy that agents of English and American propagandism were not to give their proselytes any money, *there would not be one single Protestant in Italy*. Yet, of course, they are only Protestants *in name*.

our clergy. Torn with remorse and anguish after he had touched the price of his apostasy, he said to his wife, who also had yielded to the tempter: 'Indeed, woman, I have my doubts about a religion that gives money to make itself accepted.'

"In the face of these well-known facts will the *Committee on Evangelization* still maintain that no money is given by their party for the purpose of making proselytes?"

Here we should give statistics; but it would be stepping beyond the bounds of a simple talk. Everywhere the same process, and everywhere the strong pleading of "cash" to *hold fast* the Catholic poor. "Not a day," say the "Annals of Geneva," "not a day, but we hear of some conquest by the *god of mammon*. Here a well-known minister offers work to the laborer whom he meets on the road,—work and help for the winter; there a noble lady entraps a servant in her carriage to explain the precious benefits of the Reformation; elsewhere a gentleman of some sort, who, once foiled, returns by stealth and steals from a father his children whom he sends to some Protestant asylum, etc." * Every-

---

* The "Annals," quoted above, add by way of a note: "We should mention Messrs. Oltramare, Jacquet, and Bordier

where officious and persevering visits, and the circumstance of the priest being poor is improved upon, and the faith of simple souls is ruined. "How is it?" they will say, with a look of wonder, to the wretch already soured by want, "do not your priests take care of you? Well, never mind, come to see us; we'll do something for you." Then a little talk about the wicked priests, and the abuses of the Catholic Church; the which is followed by a piece of money slipped into the poor man's hand, and oh, the glory of having gained a glorious evangelic campaign! A Christian that will go to mass no more, shall no more make his Easter, will hate the priest, — a great gain in the cause of the *pure gospel!*

Such is this ever-increasing Protestant propagandism. Such are these immoral *conversions*, no less shameful for those who procure than for those who undergo them. Sensible people among Protestants as well as among Catholics will scarcely believe such *trade in souls;* and yet it is beyond all doubt that money has become the principal agent of such propagandism. In its hands, charity is not a disinterested work;

(Protestant ministers in Geneva), who have not the least fear to become highly prominent in such visits to poor Catholics."

it is the first advance made towards apostasy: You are poor, come to us; we'll give you plenty.

How bitter that bread must taste which is bought at the price of such infamy!

In the track of this religious *stock-jobbing* the grand ideas of honor and morality, already so weakened, keep on dwindling away, grow fainter and fainter: hearts become debased, characters lose their strength, convictions crumble away; truth and religion are only a means to draw wealth out of the rich and humble the poor.

"To buy" and "to sell,"—such are the last words of Protestant propagandism.

XII. A RELIGION OF CASH.— 1. A *religion of money* is the name given to the Catholic religion by certain Protestant ministers. In concert with the scoffers of religion they charge our priests with selling holy things and trafficking on the credulity of the people, to the profit of their pockets.

It is a cunning charge. Nine out of every ten men are very sensitive whenever the dollar is touched, and to accuse the priests with love of money and intent to pilfer it from the poor, will go a great length to impair their ministry. Protestants know this; hence they repeat the charge over and over with an exceedingly bad faith; inasmuch as they should be the last to utter such an accusation.

It is not generally known that the place of a parson is a most profitable one.* The government in France gives fifteen hundred francs to a parson in the smallest villages, and a salary far larger to those in cities. Beside this emolument, they receive *perquisites*, which, although not regulated by a tariff, are none the less exacted by custom. Nor is their amount little. Fees for marriages and baptisms in Protestant churches amount to a round sum; bountiful remunerations are given for funeral services, etc.

Add to all this the never-ceasing subscriptions poured into the treasury of biblical and other societies, out of which fat salaries are taken to support their apostles. In 1856, at an Assembly of the Protestant Propaganda, in Germany, it was averred that to their agents in France alone the Association had paid *eight millions*.

Lastly, it should be remembered that in Protestant countries young ministers generally con-

---

* I have it from the very lips of a minister that the smallest salary of a parson in Paris is 15,500 francs. The amount expended by the American Board of Foreign Missions to support their agents, wives, and children is fabulous.

tract very good matrimonial alliances. It has
even been a source of complaint in certain parishes. Not long ago, in one of the cantons of
Zurich, at a meeting of young unmarried men it
was resolved that in future no unmarried minister should be accepted, "for they carry away
the best chances of the place." In other localities pastoral Presbyterial Councils, being
mainly composed of fathers of families who have
daughters to marry, obstinately refused to receive ministers already married, whose hearts
and hands were, therefore, out of market.

Now, of all the money that finds its way into
the minister's pocket not a penny is ever spent
for church service.

A temple once built (and of course it is not
the parson who builds it) requires no other care
than that of being swept once a week; there
are no sacred vestments to take care of, no expensive luminaries, no religious pomps. The
black robe of the parson is called into requisition only on Sunday; it will last a long time
with so little wear and tear, and when it is become the worse for wear it can be made available for many domestic purposes.

2. The Catholic parish priest receives from
the government a little above one-half of the
salary allowed to Protestant ministers, who are

so loud in their denunciation against the *religion of money*, eight hundred and fifty francs to priests occupying places of equal degree with those for which Protestant parsons receive fifteen hundred.

But whilst the Protestant parson is under no expense as regards church service, different is the case with the Catholic priest. In the ritual of the Christian worship there exists a material portion which entails large expenses even in the humblest churches. In the smallest country chapel the celebration of the divine service needs a supply of bread and wine, lamps and candles, sacerdotal vestments of different colors, sacred vessels, linen of various qualities; in a word such an amount of indispensable articles as would astonish those not acquainted with such details. Then you have to pay those who are employed in the Church, generally workmen who live by their labor. Besides all this the parish priest stands, by reason of his position, the first and main help of all the poor, and of all charitable undertakings in his parish. Should ever his heart be faint, his duty and his position would spur him on to act. But after all, he must live, and feed himself and the servant who waits on him.

It requires very little fairness to acknowledge that the Church is perfectly justified in authorizing our priests to levy a kind of tax on the performance of certain acts of their ministry, in order to make up for the great disproportion between their salary and their necessary expenses. They are called "perquisites." Their necessity is easily perceived. Before 1792, the perquisites in France amounted to very little indeed: no payment was required for *seats;* and the little which the priest expected at the hands of the faithful was to maintain the *right* which the priest has to live on the altar, and to receive from the Christians temporal assistance in exchange for the spiritual benefits bestowed on them by their ministrations.

"If we have sown for you spiritual things, is it a great matter if we reap your carnal things?" says St. Paul (1 Cor. ix. 11), *not meaning, of course, a compensation, which would be simony, but a necessary maintenance.* Again, "Know ye not that they who work in the sanctuary eat of the things which are of the sanctuary: and they who serve the altar partake of the altar?" (Ib. 13.)

In France, as well as under the government of Florence, and under that of the czar, and of the Emperor of Austria, the revolution has *set everything right;* they have taken everything from the Church; they could not kill her, but they have robbed her of everything in hope that she may die of starvation. She does not die, but her priests must depend on the continued liberality of the faithful for their support. Hence the necessity of pew-rents; hence the necessity, so painful to the clergy, of often calling on the people for contributions, which scarcely provide for the most necessary wants.

Do you call that a *money-making religion?*

But there *is* a money-making religion, members whereof make their millions every year, gathered from public and secret associations; and then, with a well-lined purse in hand, they climb to the attics of our mechanics, enter the huts of our peasants, take advantage of poverty and misfortune, and buy souls at their valuation of silver!

Shame on them for practising that whereof they accuse us!

XIII. A NOVEL PROOF IN FAVOR OF PROTESTANTISM. — Whilst Protestantism loses shred after shred, torn by the ruggedness of its own road, the remnants of truth and Christianity received from the Church, it becomes more and more *materialistic;* it approaches more closely to Luther's ideal, — Luther, its first apostle, — and shouts with him, "Let us eat, and let us drink, and let's be merry!"

Amongst such as have lost the faith by the Reformation, there are nations — England at the head of all, — which, by their geographical position, or their commercial talents, manage their affairs and play their cards well, make plenty of money, enjoy all the pleasures of this life, such pleasures as are now-a-days considered the only and last destiny of man. Now, will it be believed that men in their sober senses, *ministers of the gospel*, draw therefrom an argument against the Catholic Church? But so it is: "Protestants are better off than Catholics; therefore the religion of the former is the best."

A French minister, the writer of a large number of tracts, has made the above argument the subject of a whole book, which enjoyed a few days' popularity. But the author came to a sore end of it. For the "Journal des Debats," a paper not at all in the interest of Catholicity, has demolished the work and broken the argument beyond any hope of life.

Read now: —

"'*Catholic and Protestant Nations Considered, under the threefold Aspect of Prosperity, Enlightenment, and Morality; by Napoleon Rous-*

sel, a Minister.' When we opened this book we hoped to be able to write in its favor. But, in spite of the best intentions, we cannot view it as a good book or as a good act. The author has written a book, the key-note whereof is the most stupid and most demoralizing materialism. Indeed, if a *minister of the gospel* has no other moral, but such, to present to the world; if Protestant or Catholic, he can draw no better conclusion from the reading of history, then there is nothing left for man to do but have a good time, good eating, and good drinking; and the more money you have the better man you'll be; — such reading chokes the heart.

" Mr. Roussel intended to institute a comparison between Catholic and Protestant nations under the threefold relation of prosperity, enlightment, and morality. Unfortunately, in such comparison, *morality*, which should take the head place, occupies only the last and the smallest; then comes the *enlightenment:* but *well-being* stands at the head of all, as announced. . .

" In two volumes does Mr. Roussel demonstrate, with many figures, that Protestants are in this world more happy than Catholics; that they have larger incomes, possess more stock, richer silver sets at table, more shirts, and a larger assortment of shoes. Until now we have believed that, at the last judgment, God would place the good on one side and the wicked on the other; but, according to Mr. Roussel, mankind will be divided into two different classes, — the *fat* and the *lean*. God shall no more search the hearts and the reins, but the bellies of men. Were Mr. Roussel to give Saint Peter the keeping of the gates of heaven, he would give as a countersign that no person should enter unless of elegant manners and well dressed: Protestant theology requires, in order to be saved, *that a decent dress is indispensable*. . . .

"It is worth its while to see how self-pleased Mr. Roussel is in squaring up the accounts of Catholic countries and of Protestant countries: it is a regular keeping of books in Double Entry.

"On the ground of temporal welfare Mr. Roussel and Protestantism are the masters; they are the wealthiest. Compare, for instance, sad and beggared Ireland with her Protestant sisters! Mr. Roussel exhibits, from official reports, the schedule of a parish of four thousand inhabitants, *all Catholics*, — a circumstance he takes particular pains to have noted down. Now these four thousand Catholics own, between all, one cart, one plough, sixteen harrows, eight saddles for men, two side-saddles, seven table-forks, ninety-six jaunting-cars, two hundred and forty-three stools, twenty-seven geese, three turkeys, two mattresses, eight ticks, eight brass candlesticks, three watches, one school, one priest, *but* no hats, no clock, no boots, no turnips, and no carrots. . . . A stop to this catalogue. Mr. Roussel goes on whole pages; and, after having thus gone his round of the hospital, he exclaims, with a feeling of triumph: 'Let us cross the Channel, and after having visited Catholic Ireland and her misery, let us examine Protestant Scotland and her prosperity.'

"Like those who have the jaundice, and to whom every object appears tinted in yellow, Mr. Roussel unearths things from depths into which none would think he could penetrate. Proceeding in his tour he pits Catholic Switzerland against Switzerland Protestant. Here you have a traveller who arrives in a Catholic canton and at once exclaims: 'How nasty! how yellow, black, and livid they look!' Then no doubt about it: all Catholics are yellow. But here is another impression: 'We arrived in about two hours at Fluelen: this hold of Catholicism was announced by four people with goitres, six more who had the itch, and yet half a dozen ragged fellows who seemed to come out of the grave. . . .' You see how things improve in his journey; at first the Catholics were *yellow*, but then they all have the *itch*. Let us turn from such saddening sight, and look to the bright vista of a Protestant land: 'Oh, what dales! what a cultivation!' exclaims Mr. Roussel. 'What abundance! what industry! Zurich and its beautiful environs appear to me like the abode of wisdom, of moderation, of comfort, and of happiness. . . . We entered a cabin, and were presented by its mistress with milk and cherries, who also laid on the table nine or ten silver spoons. . . .' Mind it well: ten silver spoons! Oh, what a holy people! Those *yellow* Catholics, and *livid* peasants could never show the like! No, indeed! But do you fancy to follow Mr. Roussel into Spain? Even there, by dint of many quotations, he will prove to your heart's content that the roads are out of repair, the inns are dirty, and people must eat on pewter plates. Then, oh, what a contrast between that country and England, that land of Protestantism, endearing itself by its silver plate, railroads, white line, etc.!

"But we are not bound to follow Mr. Roussel in all his peregrinations; we do not doubt the accuracy of his statements, and we allow his Protestantism the benefit of its silver ware. At the same time did he not feel some compunction as he was wending his way through Ireland? Did he ever ask himself whether the Protestants were not somewhat to be blamed for the misery which harrows that Catholic country? If the Protestants represent only one-tenth of the population, what right have they to lay their hands on the whole property and revenues of the Catholic Church? But when Mr. Roussel attempts to show that Catholics are no more oppressed in Ireland, because there are four archbishops, twenty-three bishops,* two thousand five hundred churches, more than two thousand priests in Ireland, was he so insensible to every notion of admiration for a people who yet out of their poverty support their Church, whilst Protestant prelates and ministers live on the fat of the land, and enjoy all the profits of confiscation? . . .

"But Mr. Roussel's most luminous and most irresistible arguments are kept in reserve for France. Hear him at once: 'Persecuted for ages past, robbed of all they had, French Protestants ought to be to-day, not on a level, but under all the rest in point of wealth. Is it not so?

---

* Roussel should on this day add one cardinal, more bishops, more priests, more churches, and make the argument even more forcible against himself.

Were we to consult only public opinion, we might say that the reader's conscience has already given its verdict. . . . ' Please observe the queer office that *conscience* has to fill up here. But let him continue: 'We do not intend to make any assertion, even with evidence before our eyes, unless we can rest on arguments; and those we have presented on this matter are all authentic and of the gravest bearing on the question. . . . ' Here, we have trembled for Catholicity. What is coming? What thunder is going to fall on its head? Let us breathe freely! It is a bag of dollars,— a shower of big coppers. Mr. Roussel informs us that he has secured an abstract of the taxes on personal property paid by the Protestants in the Department of the Seine. The list is stereotyped; he holds it in his hand, and, on such basis, he avers that the average amount paid by all the inhabitants of Paris is *thirty-three francs, fourteen centimes;* whereas, what is paid, on an average, by the Protestants is *eighty-seven francs, one centeme;* whereupon he remarks: 'French Protestants own three times as much wealth as their Roman Catholic countrymen.' Catholicity must knock under at such a blow. Undoubtedly it will never get over this statement of the tax on personal property. But why did not

Mr. Roussel, while busy in adding and subtracting, why did he not examine another book of taxes, — those paid by a class of people whom certainly we do not wish to offend, but who pay very considerable taxes for personal property, — we mean the Jews? In that case he would have found the Israelites far more rich, and accordingly far more virtuous, than the Protestants.

"Once more, we do not wish to contradict Mr. Roussel's statement, nor mar his happiness. Let him stand, in his glory, on the top of his pyramid built by blocks of dollars and cents, and shout *Gloria in Excelsis*. SOME ONE has said that *it is easier for a camel to pass through the eye of a needle than for a rich man to enter into the kingdom of God*. We might make one or two more quotations far better to the point than those of Mr. Roussel; but it is not our province to write a sermon. Perhaps it was an honest wish of Mr. Roussel to write a moral and religious book; but a sectarian spirit has blinded him, and to our regret we must repeat that the conclusions he comes to are essentially materialistic [Signed.]

"J. LEMOINNE."

XIV. HOW CATHOLICS AND PROTESTANTS

OBSERVE SUNDAY. — A comparison often made between the strict observance of the *Sabbath* in Protestant England and its disregard in many of the largest cities of France has led to conclusions in behalf of Protestantism.

Now, beside the fact that French cities can no longer be considered as Catholic cities, the difference in question arises from the fact that in England, and in Protestant cities, the civil law lends its aid to the law religious, and employs its power to preserve the quiet of the Lord's day. Protestantism has nothing to do with it; has no merit in it. In fact, Protestants who live in places where there exists no such law, as in France, observe the Sunday not a whit better than bad Catholics. On the other hand, in Catholic countries, such as Spain and Italy, where the civil law works hand-in-hand with the religious, Sunday is observed as strictly as in London, Basle, or Geneva. Add to this that, in Protestant countries, there are also many Catholics who, subjected to the same law, no more violate the Lord's day than their Calvinistic or Anglican neighbors. Then, the rigid observance of the Sabbath in England and in Switzerland is merely a local fact; it is the happy working of a civil law, not a deep religious feeling. Were such a law to be enacted in France, those who now violate the sanctity of Sunday, for want of a spirit of faith, would act as the generality of unbelieving Englishmen do; they would observe it out of respect for authority or fear of the police.

It is worth its while to remember that this observance of the *Sabbath*, — in which, after all, the only Protestant *worship* consists, — not only has no foundation in the Bible, but it is in flagrant contradiction with its letter, which commands rest on the Sabbath, which is Saturday. It was the Catholic Church which, by the authority of Jesus Christ, has transferred this rest to the Sunday in remembrance of the resurrection of our Lord. Thus the observance of *Sunday* by the Protestants is an homage they pay, in spite of themselves, to the authority of the Church.

I shall conclude by observing that the Lord's day is observed with far more intelligence and Christian freedom by true Catholics than by Protestants. In London, the playing of music in one's house is forbidden; children are forbidden to play with marbles, or hoops; all public monuments are shut up; a promenade is looked upon as improper. It is pharisaism, not fidelity.

XV. The Conduct of Protestants towards the Mother of God.—It is a very queer way of honoring the son by insulting and despising his mother. Now, the Blessed Virgin is the mother of Jesus Christ; yet all Protestant sects join together to lay her aside with a disdain often amounting to spite and indignation.*

It is a shameful conduct, and nothing, even on Protestant principles, can excuse it.

Mary is the Mother of Jesus; but Jesus is God; therefore, Mary is the Mother of God. Passing strange that men who call themselves Christians refuse to honor the Mother of the God of Christians — her who has given us this God-Saviour! Passing strange, indeed, that subjects who call themselves faithful and devoted to this Sovereign should deny his Mother reverence and honor!

The angel appearing to the Virgin Mary, to obtain her consent for the grand mystery of the Incarnation, addressed her in words of most respectful affection: "Hail, full of grace! . . . Blessed art thou among women!"

The Catholic follows the example of the good and faithful angel, who honors the Mother of his God; whereas, Protestants prefer to follow

---

* See proceedings of the late Pan-Anglican Synod.

the lead of the false and unfaithful fallen angel, — him of whom GOD hath said from the beginning: "I will put enmity between thee and the woman... She shall crush thy head!" (Gen. iii.)

When the Holy Virgin, bearing the Redeemer of the world, *entered into the house of Zachariah, and saluted Elizabeth,* the latter *was filled with the Holy Spirit, and she cried out with a loud voice, and said:* " ... Whence is this to me, that THE MOTHER OF MY LORD should come to me? Blessed art thou among women, and blessed is the fruit of thy womb."

We Catholics follow the example of St. Elizabeth, and, led by the inspiration of the same spirit of truth, we love to attest our gratitude, our veneration, and our affection for MARY. The Protestant sects follow the senseless people of Bethlehem, who, whilst looking for the coming of Messiah, refused to receive MARY; ignoring that it was she, and she alone, who bore JESUS the Messiah!

To the homage paid to her by Elizabeth, Mary hymned the canticle of her triumphs: "*Henceforth all generations will call me blessed because the Mighty One has done great things for me.*" *

---

* In raising her to so high a dignity. (Abp. Kenrick.)

Now, who are these generations, which, fulfilling this prophecy,—this word of the Bible,—give MARY the appellation of BLESSED?

Are they the Catholics, who, in the crypts of the catacombs as well as under the domes of the most magnificent churches, sing hymns of praise to the *Blessed Name* of Mary? Or, are they the Protestant generations, who have for the Blessed Virgin neither respect nor praise, and who believe they honor her enough if they insult her not?*

Nothing clearer, nothing more glorious for MARY than these words of Holy Writ. But Protestants will still oppose to them certain words of our Lord to his Mother, — words so mysterious that no one can fathom their depth, and which aim at naught else but to make MARY share in the annihilation of the Redemption, as she had from the beginning partaken of the joys and glories of the Incarnation.

Were these words to be taken according to † Protestant, interpretation, we must needs con-

---

* A dignitary of the Episcopal Church has said from one of our Boston pulpits that "Mary, after all, was no more than any other woman."

† Some Protestants, actually maniacs in their hatred for MARY, have even attacked her perpetual virginity (to say nothing of those who have called her an adulteress); because

clude that JESUS did not love his Mother, honored her not, and was a bad son, and violated the fourth commandment of his own law, to wit: "Thou shalt honor thy father and thy mother." Who wishes to prove too much proves nothing. *Qui nimium probat, nihil probat.*

After his Father in heaven, our Lord loved none so intensely as he did his mother. Besides her being his mother, she is the humblest, the purest, the holiest of all creatures. Thus JESUS loved MARY with a love peculiar to himself. In our love and respect for MARY we conform ourselves to the sentiments of JESUS, and practise also, although very imperfectly, the great rule laid down by St. Paul, "*Have this mind in yourselves, which also was in* CHRIST JESUS;" that is, love what Christ hath loved (Ph. ii. 5).

there are passages in the gospel making allusion to some *brothers* of the Lord. Have they not heard that in the East, even in our own days, the name of *brother* is given to the nearest of kin? Oriental languages have not a word to express the relationship of cousin; and the Bible, among other instances, introduces Abraham, addressing his *nephew*, Lot, thus: "*Let there be no quarrel, I beseech thee, between me and thee; . . . for we are brethren.*" (Gen. xiii. 8.) St. James, who was a cousin-german of our Saviour, is often called brother of the Lord.

The dogma of the perpetual virginity of MARY is confirmed by all the monuments of the apostolic times. Whoever dares to dispute its truth is devoid of Christian feeling, has no Christian decency.

We invoke the Blessed Virgin in our wants, because we know that she has power over the heart of her Son, and that the first of our Saviour's miracles was performed at the request of his mother.

As the Father has given us JESUS through MARY, so also he willeth that all the gifts of JESUS should come to us through the same channel. Mary is *not* our *mediatrix of redemption*,— CHRIST JESUS alone has ransomed us and saved us. But she is a mediatrix by intercession, by tender affection for us; she is our advocate, our adopted mother. We beg her protection near the good GOD, just as a child flies to its mother to interest her to obtain what it wishes from the father.

In fact, the honor Christians pay to MARY ascends direct to JESUS CHRIST: the Son is honored in his Mother. We love and praise MARY, because we wish to congratulate her on her being the mother of JESUS, and to thank her because she has given Him to us. The worship of *honor* rendered by us to MARY is a safeguard to the worship of *adoration* which we are bound to render to JESUS, and what we witness every day is a triumphant proof of our assertion. For it is reserved for the Catholic Church, accused as she is of forgetting JESUS for the sake of

MARY, — the Creator for the creature, — it is reserved for her alone to hold up and defend against Protestant infidelity the divinity of that only Mediator, of whose honor heresy hypocritically feigns to be so jealous, and yet denies his Divine Nature every day.*

XVI. PROTESTANTISM IS DISHEARTENING. — GOD is the Maker of both the heart of man and of the Catholic Church; and GOD has made the Catholic Church wonderfully adapted to all the needs and requirements of the human heart.†

Her doctrinal authority meets our wants for a belief, for without authority there is no faith. The ceremonies of her ritual satisfy our nature, composed as it is of body and soul, and needing to blend material elements to the purely spiritual acts of her adorations. Confession fills

---

* AUGUSTUS NICOLAS has published a work entitled, "Philosophical Studies on the Blessed Virgin. — The Virgin Mary and the Divine Plan. — The Virgin Mary in the Gospel. — The Virgin Mary living in the Church." All the difficulties raised against the worship of the Mother of God are peremptorily met and demolished. Said an enlightened magistrate: "Mr. Nicolas, no Protestant can remain such after reading your book."

† See "The Functions of the Subjective in Religion," by Very Rev. W. H. Anderdon, D. D., M. A., Oxon., in "The Catholic World," Nov., 1867, pp. 175, etc.

the want of penance and mercy,— a want felt at the very bottom of the sinful soul. The invocation of saints, the prayers offered for the departed souls, foster the sentiment of eternal union of souls with GOD and of solidarity of men among themselves,— and so on with all the dogmas, all the precepts, and all the practices of the Church.

Protestantism is cold, formal, naked, just like the walls of its temples, wherein only the absence of GOD is felt.

Oh, the poor soul, estranged or wilful, who, like the prodigal son in the Gospel, quits the father's home to wander over the distant and dismal lands of error!— once out of the bracing atmosphere wherein GOD had, in his mercy, placed her birth, she breathes only in a frozen blast, and finds naught but void and desolation.

As for him who becomes a Protestant, no hope of control when passion rages, yet great comfort at the moment he repents,— no guide when doubt tosses him about, yet a more bountiful pardon after his fall, a more merciful confessor to console him, and to pardon him in the name and with the authority of GOD. Poor apostate! for him no more the beautiful ceremonies of the Church. The images of our Lord, of the Blessed Virgin, and of the saints, become emblems of idolatry!—no more crucifix, no more the sign of the cross: it is idolatry!—no more prayers; no more respect or love for the Mother of GOD: idolatry!—no more trusting the intercession of saints, patrons in heaven, advocates, protectors near GOD: idolatry!

And when the hour of death is drawing near,—when the unfortunate *man is left to himself*, about standing before GOD covered with the sins of his whole life,—no priest to administer the last sacraments of the Church, no priest to tell him with all the power of divine authority, "Poor sinner, take courage; thou canst die in peace, because JESUS has given me the power to forgive thee thy sins, and I pardon thee in his name."

Nor is this all. The apostate's body shall not be carried to the Church; it shall be carried straight on to an unblessed place of burial,—unblessed, because such benedictions are only idolatry in the eyes of Protestants. Lastly, if his children have turned Protestants like their father, they are forbidden to pray for their father; for, Protestantism admits neither purgatory nor prayers for departed souls: it is all idolatry. No, that dreary worship will not allow a prayer for the poor dead, nor a compassionate visit to their last dwelling-place. Some impotent and unfelt tears when the last sod of earth falls on the coffin, and it is all over between them and ourselves!

As for myself, I must say, this one thought would be ample proof to convince me of the absolute falseness of Protestantism. The want of praying for those whom we have loved and lost, is so deep-felt, so peremptory, so natural to man's heart, that a religion denying its being met, and forbidding its being filled, is condemned in advance.

She only expressed a universal sentiment, that poor little girl of ten years old, when beside the dead body of her mother, she said to me with a wonderful determination: "When I am grown up, and will have become the mistress of my own actions, I'll be a Catholic: I do not wish to be of a creed which forbids me to love the Holy Virgin and to pray for my mother."

XVII. THE JUDGMENT OF DEATH. — It has been remarked that death is the echo of life. At the solemn approach of death sophisms lose their force, illusions melt away, and conscience asserts its rights. During the process entered by Protestants against the Church, let us appeal to the verdict of a supreme authority, — the verdict of death.

There are Protestants who have become Catholics, and there are Catholics who have turned Protestants. Let us watch and see how they die.

At death's point, as well as during their lives, the numberless Protestants who have re-entered the pale of the Church were full of hope and in a most serene state of mind; not a word of regret from their lips, not the least remorse to ripple the tranquillity of their souls, not a doubt to give them the least anxiety. They believe, and love, and pray, and give up their souls to God, with thanks because he has received them in the Catholic Church! I defy all the Protestants in the world to quote one single instance in contradiction to this statement.

All those doctors, and ministers, and men highly educated and perfectly independent, who, raised in Protestantism, and knowing it to its very depth, have abandoned it to become Catholics, — all, without a single exception, die, like the illustrious Count de Stolberg, the greatest among them, full of joy and love of God, blessing Him because He had led him to know His true Church, and beseeching his children to pray for the dead, and to persevere in the Catholic Church. After receiving the last sacraments in the most humble attitude, he died with these words on his lips: "Blessed be Jesus Christ!"

How different the death of apostates! Even when not lost to every sentiment of faith in GOD and in an immortal soul, — even when not hardened into materialism and atheism, — what anxiety, what pangs of conscience, what terrors toss them on the pillow of death! Then they remember that holy Church they have forsaken, and why they have forsaken it! The world, with all its endearments and charms, fades away from before their eyes aghast at the approaching sight of judgment and eternity! Yea; if the least belief in the Holy Scripture is still alive in their hearts, they remember Christ's words, "*What doth it profit a man if he gain the whole world and lose his soul?*"

The death-bed of the founders of Protestantism — all apostates, and, for the most, apostate priests — bears us out in our assertion, and with a terribly overwhelming evidence.

Luther despaired of the salvation of his soul. Shortly before his death, his concubine pointed to the brilliancy of the stars in the firmament.

"See, Martin, how beautiful that heaven is!"

"It does not shine in our behalf," replied the master, moodily.

"Is it because we have broken our vows?" resumed Kate, in dismay.

"May be," said Luther.

"If so, let us go back."

"Too late! The hearse is stuck in the mire," — and he would hear no more.

At Eisleben, on the day previous to that on which he was stricken with apoplexy, he remarked to his friends: "I have almost lost sight of the Christ, tossed as I am by these waves of despair which overwhelm me." And after a while, "I, who have imparted salvation to so many, cannot save myself."

Above I have quoted his blasphemous testament. He died forlorn of GOD, — blaspheming to the very end. His last word was an attestation of impenitence. His eldest son, who had doubts both about the Reformation and the Reform, asked him for a last time whether he persevered in the doctrine he preached. "Yes," replied a gurgling sound from the old sinner's throat, — and Luther was before his GOD! *

Schusselburg, a Protestant, writes: "Calvin died of scarlet fever, devoured by vermin, and eaten up by an ulcerous abscess, the stench whereof drove away every person." — (*Theol. Calvin.* t. ii. p. 72.) In great misery he gave up his rascally ghost, despairing of salvation,

---

* The last descendant of Luther died not long ago a fervent Catholic.

evoking the devils from the abyss, and uttering oaths most horrible and blasphemies most frightful.

John Hazen, a disciple of Calvin and an eye-witness of his death, writes thus: "Calvin died in despair. He died a death hideous and revolting, such as GOD has threatened the impious and reprobate with."—(*De vita Calvini*.) And he adds, "I can vouch for the truth of what I say, because I have been an eye-witness."

Spalatin, Justus Jonas, Isinder, and a host of other friends of Luther, died either in despair or crazy.

Henry VIII. died bewailing that he had lost heaven; and his worthy daughter Elizabeth breathed her last in deep desolation, stretched on the floor,—not daring to lie in bed, because, at the first attack of her illness, she thought she saw her body all torn to pieces and palpitating in a caldron of fire.

Let, then, in the presence of such frightful deaths and of the thought of eternity, those of our unfortunate brethren who may be tempted to abandon their Church, remember that a day will come when they will also be summoned to appear before GOD! Let them think, in their sober senses, of death and of judgment and of hell, and I pledge my word they will not think of becoming Protestants.

In a place upon the borders of Northern Germany there formerly lived a priest who had become careless of all the duties of his state. Falling from excess into excess, he went so far as to deny his faith, and, fleeing his native place, he became a Protestant. Then he secured a place, and from a teacher of truth he became a teacher of false doctrines. Many years did the unfortunate man remain in that state of enmity with his God. On a certain occasion he was the guest of a famous preacher in a large city, who had gathered around his table many pastors of the neighborhood. Amid the enjoyments of the table, word was sent to the master that a poor man had fallen dangerously ill, and seemed to be in great need of spiritual assistance. The pastor, bound to entertain his guests, could not attend the call, and our apostate offered his services in his stead. The offer was accepted, and he went. He was led to a chamber where lay an old man at the point of death, and in utmost despair of his salvation. The parson read to him some passages from the Scriptures; but to all the dying man replied, "I am lost — no pardon for me — woe to me! I am damned!"

The visitor endeavored to comfort him and to inspire him with feelings of confidence.

"No use," replied the other, "no use; no one can give me help; the road to heaven is closed against me; my crime is too great; I am lost!"

"But, for the love of GOD, why so? What is it that weighs on your heart so heavily?"

The dying man replied only by words of despair. At last he gave in to the pastor's remonstrances, and said, "What renders my case hopeless is that I am an apostate priest, and then the crimes I have added to my apostasy, and my resisting so much to the graces of God, and to all the advances of the divine mercy, which I have repelled... Alas! it is too great a sin for me to sue for pardon; I am lost; none can bring aid to me!"

The disclosure threw the visitor's soul into a cruel agony, as he recognized in the sick man his own fearful destiny. But his former faith worked again in his heart, as he thought of the divine and inamissible power given to the priest in the Sacrament of Order. Accordingly he addressed the wretched man with great feeling thus: "Dear brother, I can aid you, as sure as God exists; I can give you aid!... I, also, am a Catholic priest, believe me; but, alas! I am like yourself a renegade and excommunicated; but, with the priestly power I possess, I can open the gates of heaven to a dying man."

The wretched man felt as if an angel had come from heaven to give him hope and salvation. Overwhelmed by such a proof of the infinite mercy of his GOD, who, at the very last hour of his life, offered him pardon, and with pardon the renewal of all former favors, and an assurance of salvation, with sentiments of a most vivid sorrow and most sincere repentance, he made a confession of his sins, received absolution, and died in the peace of the Lord. Such a triumph of the divine love, that wishes the salvation of all men, and goes in quest of the worst sinners to their very last breath, made such an impression on him who had been chosen to achieve it, and his heart was at once so changed by the all-powerful grace of GOD, that he resolved to retrace his steps. Accordingly as he re-entered the hall where his clerical friends were still enjoying the feast, he addressed them thus: "Gentlemen, farewell! I am going back to the bosom of the Catholic Church, that I have so wantonly abandoned. I have just witnessed how horrible is the death of an apostate. I found myself to be a priest still, and I have been an instrument of mercy in in the hands of GOD; and now that very infinite mercy calls me also to repentance, to reconciliation, and to salvation. Farewell!"*

XVIII. PROTESTANTISM AND INFIDELITY.— The infidels and rationalists of our times greatly sympathize with Protestantism and the work of the Reformation; they look upon Luther and Calvin as their grandsires, and they have reason for it. Protestants who still remain Christians will deny it, yet it is a fact that the infidelity which rends modern society is the fatal but logical consequence of the religious rebellion of the sixteenth century.

The Protestant rejects, on the claim of private

---

* Rev. Dr. Wharton, who died in 1832 (?), minister of a Protestant church at Elizabethtown, N. J., was born of an ancient Catholic family in Maryland related to the famous Carrolls, became a Jesuit, professed in that order, and in 1774 apostatised in Worcester, England. He married twice. "Poor old Dr. Wharton is continually tortured by his conscience. His cook at the parsonage house near Trenton, New Jersey, a good Irish Catholic, fell dangerously sick, and, as no priest could be procured, Wharton said to her: 'Although I am a parson, I am also a Catholic priest, and can give you absolution in your case.' She made her confession and he absolved her." Père Grivel, who wrote this letter May 30, 1832, had this account from Mr. Wharton's nephew, a good Catholic, and a magistrate in Washington. Shortly after, the unhappy man was summoned before the tribunal of GOD.

judgment, a part of the Christian truths which the Church teaches to the world by the authority of Christ. The infidel, in the name of the same freedom, goes farther and rejects *all* Christian truths.

The Protestant rejects the Church because he does not believe it to be of divine institution. The infidel rejects Christ because he does not believe him to be really GOD.

It is the same principle with both. It is the individual reason which takes the place of faith, that is, of the submission of the spirit to divine authority. The Protestant, whether he believes it or not, is an infidel in germ, and the infidel is a Protestant in full bloom.*

Infidelity exists in Protestantism as the oak exists in the acorn, as the consequence is in the premise. Down the road of negation the descent is very steep and slippery. If the freedom of judgment in a Lutheran, or his reason, or the view he takes, as you may be better pleased to call it, leads him to reject the authority of the Pope, Vicar of Jesus Christ, that same

---

* In 1852 we remember a distinguished American reviewer to assert that he knew only *two consistent* Protestants, to wit: Dr. Parker and Father Lampson. Our Boston friends, who must well remember the eccentricities of the latter, will at once see the point.

free judgment leads the Calvinist to reject the real presence of our Lord in the Eucharist, — a dogma, however, preserved by the Lutherans. According to the same principle, the Socinians, the ministers at Geneva, and a crowd of other ministers, following the footsteps of Voltaire and Rousseau, reject to-day the divinity of Jesus Christ, and therefore abjure Christianity and fall back into utter incredulity; and all in consequence of that freedom of conscience. But our German and French philosophers, rationalists and pantheists of all degrees, do not even stop at that,—go farther, and deny the existence of a God Creator, and all by the privilege of free and private judgment.

Now, I say it again, and all Protestants must needs say it with me, this private judgment is Protestantism in its essential principle. Then Luther, the father of private judgment and of Protestantism, is the father of all infidelity, the father of all anti-Christian negation.*

Eugene Rendu, in his "Report on Public Instruction in Germany," writes: "I was in Jena two months before the opening of the Synod

---

* Such was the feeling of Henry IV. when he was a stanch Calvinist. As regards piety he found Turk and Protestant to be alike. Said he to the Marquise of Verneuil : "D— me, were I not *Huguenot*, I'll turn *Turk*."

which was to assemble in Eisenach the pastors of the different States of Germany. Said I to a distinguished professor of divinity in the University of Jena, 'Will they discuss dogmatic questions and doctrines?' 'No,' he replied, 'only liturgy and simple questions of form will be deliberated. As for the rest, *it is out of question for us to agree.* When we meet on dogmatic field, pshaw! it is all over (*pst, tout disparait!*)'"

Eugene Sue, at the head of the anti-Christian league, among a thousand other things, has written the following, which I recommend to the careful consideration of all Catholics, and all the many Protestants who love truth. He writes: "Free men, radical men, and rationalists have probably been very indiscreet in attacking Protestantism, — a sort of transitory religion, . . . a bridge, so to speak, over which we may reach a pure rationalism, at the same time allowing the false necessity of a worship, which the mass of the people will not as yet know how to do away with. . . . We, free-thinkers, well aware of dangers inherent to all religions, admit the necessity of a religion (transitory, it is true). for, we must say it, we need distinguish the possible from what is desirable. It must be acknowledged that there are several degrees in evil, and that the least thereof is preferable to the whole," * — that is, this "whole evil" is JESUS CHRIST and his Church, religion, and the Catholics.

Then passing from theory to practice, Eugene Sue draws the impious rules of an association whose members shall not baptize their children, nor marry with religious rites, nor bring their dead to the Church; in one word, will altogether renounce any and every practice of religion.

Another man, Edgar Quinet, a great herald of Protestantism, and son-in-law of a parson, † styles the Protestant sects *the thousand gates open to get out of Christianity*.

You will say, "Our Protestants generally speaking do not go so far as that." True: there are degrees in Protestantism, and absolute infidelity is only Protestantism in the highest degree.

XIX. PROTESTANTISM AND REVOLUTION. — All Protestantism is of itself revolutionist. I do not say "all Protestants," but "all Protest-

---

* Letter to "Le National Belge," in November, 1856.

† Whilst we are translating this page, is laid before us the account of sects existing this year, 1867, in London, and it sums to *ninety-five*, with an *et cætera:* among the rest that of "Countess of Huntington's Connection"!

antism," for I know very well that man is not always so consistent as to make his actions harmonize with his belief. Often he is worth more for what he does than for what he thinks. As we unfortunately meet mad revolutionists among Catholics, so we do meet Protestants who are sincere lovers of order. But here we do not deal with Protestants, but with Protestantism, and I say it again, — all Protestantism is revolutionist.

Whilst Catholicity is a submission of heart and mind to the authority of the Church, Protestantism is the negation of all authority in matters of religion.

Now, if we once admit the principle that man should not acknowledge any religious authority, is it not a simple, natural, and logical inference that he is no more bound to acknowledge a political or civil authority?

"Why should not those who have refused obedience to the Church, refuse also obedience to the State? Protestantism,—that is, the rebellion against religious authority, — contains in its bowels the seed of rebellion against all political authority.

"The history of Protestantism gives a most luminous proof of this truth. Wherever it was proclaimed, its first appeal to Christians to revolt against the Pope was immediately succeeded by an appeal to the nations to rebel against their sovereigns. The very tongues of the leaders of the Reformation, who uttered these atrocious blasphemies against the Head of the Church, belched forth afterward the bloodiest insults against the heads of the State. For such geniuses of disorder, whilst the Sovereign Pontiff was only a tyrant, princes were monsters, and the *religious wars*, which in those wretched days covered with blood the fields of Germany, England, and France, were not, after all, but *wars of revolution*.*

"Since then, Protestantism has ever sympathized with rebellions, and every rebellion has given to Protestantism its most unequivocal testimony of sympathy, Protestantism has ever been radically revolutionist, as every rebellion has essentially been Protestant.

"The spirit of rebellion, which, within a few years past, has convulsed certain Catholic countries, was begotten in the bosom of Protestant peoples. It is since the Reformation has failed to upset the altar, that thrones have been shaken to their foundation. The revolution of Catholic

---

* Our American readers are greatly mistaken, if they believe for one moment that the present wars in Italy are actually waged for the sake of liberty.

France was only a bloody repetition of the revolution of Protestant England. English Protestantism can alone claim the glory — a sad glory — of having introduced into Christian Europe the pagan fashion of assassinating kings juridically." *

Having this common origin, Protestantism and revolution meet together in one mass. Honest Protestants, it is true, repel such an union, which frightens them. Yet it is accomplished by a sort of fatality, such as influenced the principle of the Reformation, and the most outspoken organs of socialism proclaim it most loudly.

Quinet writes: "I address myself to all beliefs, to all religions, who have fought Rome: THEY ALL ARE, WHETHER THEY WILL IT OR NOT, ON OUR SIDE; for, after all, their existence is as irreconcilable as ours with the rule of Rome."

Louis Blanc says: "*Every religious Luther necessarily avers a Luther political.*"

Mazzini, Garibaldi, and those other adventurers, who some years ago held under an ignoble yoke the capital of the Christian world, found no better means to give root to, and make a

---

* Sermons preached at the Tuileries, before the Emperor, in 1857, by Fr. Ventura. 4th sermon.

social revolution thrive in Italy, than by introducing Protestantism. Thousands of falsified, spurious Bibles were distributed in Rome, and a project was on foot to give to Protestants the Church of the Pantheon, in the very heart of Rome. In 1850 Garibaldi said to the Protestant minister Pozzi, while entrusting the education of his son to him: "*The Bible is the cannon that will open Italy to us.*"

However, the shameless publications of modern revolutionists are open to the inspection of Protestants as they are to us. Let them examine them. With a unanimous voice the revolutionists applaud Protestantism, *the religious form of revolution.*

It is a fact well worth the study of serious men; it is a fact undeniable and public. Such as are indifferent to the sacred interest of faith should feel some anxiety about the dangers which threaten the domestic hearth.

"Socialism is only a Protestantism against society, as Protestantism is socialism against the Church." *

---

* Aug. Nicolas' "Du Protestantism et de toutes les Heresies dans leur rapport avec le Socialisme." It is a remarkable work and it cannot be recommended highly enough to those who wish to probe deeply the questions and truths at which we

XX. PROTESTANTISM IN CATHOLIC COUNTRIES.*— France is Catholic to the core. She has too much good sense and logic to be capable of any other religion. She may become infidel, but Protestant — never.

Whenever Protestantism met with encouragement in France, it was with the revolutionary party that had revolted against the lawful authority. If its standard ever covered Frenchmen, those Frenchmen were traitors who conspired with the foreigner and fomented civil war. If, outside of such followers, it ever rallied around its folds friends and supporters, it was because of its revolutionary idea, and such partisans do not add much to its glory.

There is nothing in Protestantism but what is repulsive to the French spirit. Protestantism contradicts itself and can stand no examination. It is stiff and unnatural: its formal authority only enacts the cold presumption of the Pharisee: it has no resources from which either reason, or the imagination, or the heart can draw.

---

have only hinted. See also on this matter Fr. Perrone's "Protestantism and the Rule of Faith."

* This last article is headed, "Le Protestantism n'est pas Francais." What the learned author says about France can as properly be applied to Spain and Italy, and all Catholic countries.

On the other hand Protestantism does not feel at home in France. What the French love, Protestantism loathes; and what the latter loves, France does not love at all. It is in England, the genuine centre of Protestantism in the world, where its fondest hopes are cherished, and may be realized, that the propagandism of France is nurtured, fed chiefly by foreign aid, probably more political in its nature than religious.

France would never countenance king or queen that were not Catholics. Henry IV., a prince so beloved by the sires of the French people, was held aloof as long as he remained a Huguenot. Never did a Protestant male or female sit on the throne of France. An attempt of this kind was made within our memory,* but GOD, who holds France in his keeping, manifested his judgment with terrible and summary punishment.

France shall cease to be herself when she will cease to be THE OLDEST DAUGHTER OF THE CHURCH!

CONCLUSION.

And now, farewell, my reader. My dear

---

* The author alludes to the Duke of Orleans, son of Louis Philippe, — the renegade son of a perjured father.

friend, pray for me, if this little work has done any good to you. Pray, also, for those who may read it.

I have addressed myself to your good sense, and to your loyalty, and I have hopes that I have made you lay your finger on the deep misery of what is called Protestantism!

Should you ever have any occasion to have a discussion with a Protestant, be cautious and charitable. Never allow yourself to be thrown out of the track of the straightforward path, clear and practical, of good sense. Enter not into fruitless questions, which are only fit, as Paul puts it, to trouble and estrange souls. Refer cavillers, quibblers, and inventors of new religions, to your parish priest.

As for yourselves, keep the faith: be docile and faithful children of the holy Catholic Church, which is the teacher of true piety, and the infallible depositary of Christian truths. Practise your faith with fervor and love: pray much and receive communion often: love with a deep-hearted love JESUS CHRIST your Saviour, the Blessed Virgin his Mother, the Pope the visible representative of your Redeemer. In a word, live so that you may, when the days of your pilgrimage on earth will be over, reach GOD and live with him forever!

www.ingramcontent.com/pod-product-compliance
Lightning Source LLC
Chambersburg PA
CBHW031353230426
43670CB00006B/534